Stacy is incredibly knowledgeable about how young children master letter recognition and early literacy skills. She has a great way of explaining the concept and she makes it so relatable. Stacy's philosophy is grounded in developmentally appropriate practices, how children learn best through play, and how engaging environments can support children is mastering letter recognition, alphabet knowledge. This book is a valuable resource for early childhood educators. I am beyond thrilled to share this book!

—Prerna Richards, *Early Childhood Consultant*

The Whole Child Alphabet provides both a holistic approach to alphabet knowledge and also specific examples of activities that can be implemented to enhance alphabet learning. Benge presents research-based, developmentally appropriate opportunities for creating environments and opportunities for learning that occur through natural processes such as play. Benge provides a solid foundation for the "why" and "how" of alphabet learning based on the cognitive and physical developmental levels of the learner. This is written in an easily accessible manner for educators, parents, and caregivers alike!

—Michelle Ciminelli, PhD, *Associate Professor, Niagara University*

In a world where so many are demanding that "earlier is better," Stacy reminds us that "Everything starts somewhere" in this practical book on early literacy development. Her extensive research coupled with personal and professional experience makes this an easy read that leads to deeper knowledge behind the "why" and improved daily practice in the "how". Every chapter has a section with simple ideas to implement in your classroom today to build literacy skills and a section to help you communicate to stakeholders that might be pushing back on best practices. This is a phenomenal training resource for new early educators and an excellent reference book for experienced educators.

—Monica Healer, *Executive Director, The Early Childhood Christian Network*

The Whole Child Alphabet: How Young Children Actually Develop Literacy by Stacy Benge is a must-read for librarians, teachers, caregivers, and parents – all those who want the best early literacy education for young children! Benge adds insightful perspectives on letter recognition, sounds, and writing alphabet knowledge. Benge's suggestions are a welcome change in pedagogy that includes incorporating a strengths-based, child-led, play-based approach to literacy in a developmentally appropriate environment. Read and discover how young children actually develop literacy, where discovery leads to a world of access and joyful development of alphabet knowledge.

—Mary Barbara Trube, EdD, *Early Childhood Specialist, Platonium Mentoring & Coaching Consultants*

THE WHOLE child ALPHABET

How Young Children Actually Develop Literacy

by Stacy Benge, M.S.

Exchange Press

ISBN 978-0-942702-85-9
eISBN 978-0-942702-86-6

©2023 Stacy Benge

Book Design: Scott Bilstad

Managing Editor: Erin Glenn

This book may not be reproduced in whole or in part by any means without written permission of the publisher. For more information about other Exchange Press publications and resources for directors and teachers, contact:

Exchange Press
7700 A Street
Lincoln, NE 68510
(800) 221-2864
ExchangePress.com

Dedication

To my parents, Dan and Brenda, who encouraged me,

To my boys, Mason and Jackson, who inspired me,

To my husband, Jason, who believed in me.

This book is dedicated to you.

WHOLE CHILD ALPHABET

Table of Contents

INTRODUCTION
The Idea 9

What is your favorite letter? 17

CHAPTER ONE
The Cornerstones of Language and Literacy 19

CHAPTER TWO
Learning the Alphabet Begins with Interest and Connection 31

CHAPTER THREE
Letter Recognition Begins with Vision 53

CHAPTER FOUR
Letter Sounds Begin with Phonemic Awareness 77

CHAPTER FIVE
Writing the Alphabet Begins with Physical Development 99

CHAPTER SIX
Alphabet Knowledge Begins with Child-Led Play 139

CHAPTER SEVEN
Moving Forward 151

CONCLUSION
Change Begins with Our Pedagogy 163

Bibliography 167

WHOLE CHILD ALPHABET

INTRODUCTION

The Idea

For the past 15 years, while either presenting professional development sessions or conducting classroom observations, I noticed an overemphasis on alphabet instruction; specifically, letter of the week themes. When I asked people why we do this in the early years, their answers usually revolved around stakeholder expectations, predetermined curriculum plans, and school readiness pressures. Often, people simply said, "It's the way we've always done it." I responded by sharing the fundamentals of language and literacy as well as foundational skills children need to be successful readers and writers - when they are developmentally ready. I talked about the importance of being child-centered and connecting the environment to the children. I described how alphabet knowledge requires the whole child – not just memorizing and tracing letters. Most of the time people agreed, but then asked afterwards, "If we don't do letter of the week, or flash cards, or worksheets, how do we teach the alphabet? And how do I explain all of this to my administrators and families?"

As a result, I started presenting a training that explains the solid base that needs to be developed before children can even attempt reading and writing. Specifically, I break down the skills needed for alphabet knowledge, including children's ability to:

- understand the purpose of the alphabet (genuine interest and print awareness)

- identify individual letters (visual perception)

- assign sounds to those letters (phonological awareness and auditory sense)

- eventually write the letters (physical development and proper letter formation).

I emphasize the importance of designing an environment that encourages child-led play to enhance and strengthen these developmental skills. I also share simple, teacher-guided activities that are interactive and developmentally appropriate. (But should never replace play!) While walking through these experiences, I continually stress that although alphabet knowledge is a critical part of the literacy process, it is a small component and not sufficient on its own. In other words, to read and write, children need more than just knowing the letters. Therefore, it is critical to pay attention to the other building blocks of literacy in the learning environment and honor their importance in the reading and writing process.

I also address having conversations with stakeholders and addressing their concerns. The biggest piece of advice I give is to learn and understand the intricacies of language and literacy development. When we do this, it helps us explain the complexities of those developmental processes and how they work together to build strong foundations for reading and writing. It is important to remember that we do not create strong readers and writers by introducing instruction at an early age. Instead, our focus needs to be on creating environments and experiences that provide opportunities for children to play and develop solid foundational skills that support literacy. Understanding and respecting children's developmental stages is crucial to the process.

As I presented this material over the years I found that people were excited to learn more, and were often interested in going deeper into language and literacy development. Many were seeking ideas to implement in the classroom. Others wanted more information to help them move away from the traditional letter of the week activities and toward a child-centered approach.

Often, people would ask if the material was available as a book. After continuously receiving this feedback, I decided to write this book. My wish is that you enjoy reading it and find it beneficial when reflecting on how you approach language, literacy, and alphabet knowledge in your setting. I hope you feel encouraged to consider child-centered practices that might go against the grain, and perhaps make some changes you had not considered before. I look forward to hearing how this book may inspire you and even transform your pedagogy.

My Viewpoint

Although I work in the realm of early childhood education, I identify more as a developmentalist, focusing on human development across the lifespan in all domains. I believe the keys to early education include understanding the intricacies of child development, building relationships with the children presently in the setting, then designing the environment, interactions, and experiences around that. This is what will bring about the strong foundations that will support children in their future endeavors, not pushing a top-down agenda and introducing academics too soon. The mindset needs to be a matter of development, not a matter of teaching.

Intended Audience

This book is intended for any professional or organization caring for children ages birth to five, including: child care centers, day care centers, child development centers, nursery schools, family child care centers, preschools, pre-k, kindergarten, elementary schools, and any setting that serves young children and their families. Regardless of label, affiliation, funding, requirements, or perception, the goal of all these programs should be the same, doing what is best and developmentally appropriate for the children presently in the setting.

Frequently, people ask "At what age should we introduce the alphabet?" My answer is, when the children presently in your setting start showing an interest in the letters. This will vary class to class and year to year, but this might start to peak around the age of four. (Or not, depending on the child.) Keep in mind, the purpose of this book is not about how to introduce and teach the alphabet but rather to look at the foundational skills needed to support alphabet knowledge. If you care for children under the age of four, this book is for you. Everything starts somewhere and for language and literacy, that starting point is at birth. Many of the chapters have sections highlighting the various developmental stages children progress through. While the sections on letter recognition and letter formation pertain to preschool age children, the majority of the material serves children from birth to 5. Use your professional judgement and follow your children's cues.

Families

If you are a family member reading this book, thank you! Although the language is directed towards educators, the information presented can benefit anyone associated with young children. The portions focusing on child development will hopefully explain the stages you will see your child progress through; rest assured, they will go at their own pace and that is okay. Understanding this information will help you advocate for the practices that are best for your child.

The experiences listed for the classroom can easily be implemented at home as well. Please take special note of the emphasis on child-led play. This is the key for children's growth and development. Nothing can replace it. So, when wondering what all you can be doing for your child at home, the best thing is providing a place for them to freely explore and play. Without a doubt, this is the greatest way for your child to develop the fundamental skills they need to support them in life.

Methods of Teaching

Instead of being mere position statements, developmentally appropriate practice, advancing equity in early childhood, and anti-bias education need to be embraced as pedagogy and methods of teaching and caregiving. Please keep this mindset for all subject matter, ideas, and applications mentioned throughout this book.

Developmentally Appropriate Practice

"NAEYC defines 'developmentally appropriate practice' as methods that promote each child's optimal development and learning through a strengths-based, play-based approach to joyful, engaged learning. Educators implement developmentally appropriate practice by recognizing the multiple assets all young children bring to the early learning program as unique individuals and as members of families and communities. Building on each child's strengths—and taking care to not harm any aspect of each child's physical, cognitive, social, or emotional well-being—educators design and implement learning environments to help all children achieve their full potential across all domains of development and across all content areas. Developmentally appropriate practice recognizes and supports each individual as a valued member of the learning community. As a result, to be developmentally appropriate, practices must also be culturally, linguistically, and ability appropriate for each child" (NAEYC, 2020).

Advancing Equity in Early Childhood

"Advancing the right to equitable learning opportunities requires recognizing and dismantling the systems of bias that accord privilege to some and are unjust to others. Advancing the full inclusion of all individuals across all social identities will take sustained efforts far beyond those of early childhood educators alone. Early childhood educators, however, have a unique opportunity and obligation to advance equity. With the support of the early education system as a whole, they can create early learning environments that equitably distribute learning opportunities by helping all children experience responsive interactions that nurture their full range of social, emotional, cognitive, physical, and linguistic abilities; that reflect and model fundamental principles of fairness and justice; and that help them accomplish the goals of anti-bias education" (NAEYC, 2019).

Anti-Bias Education

"Anti-bias education (ABE) is an optimistic commitment to supporting children who live in a highly diverse and yet still inequitable world. Rather than a formula for a particular curriculum, it is an underpinning perspective and framework that permeates everything in early childhood education – including your interactions with children, families, and colleagues. ABE is based on an understanding that children are individuals with their own personalities and temperaments and with social group identities based on the families who birth and raise them and the way society views who they are. These identities are both externally applied by the world around them and internally constructed within the child" (Derman-Sparks, Edwards, & Goins, 2020).

Terminology Notes

The intent of all terminology is respect and inclusivity. The words caregiver, educator, professional, and teacher are used interchangeably throughout the book. These terms are not governed by levels of formal education, years of experience, or ages of children in the settings. Select the title you are most comfortable with and own it, and then respect what others choose as well. Please know that when I use any of the above-mentioned terms, I am referring to a person who cares for children of all ages, designs environments for them, plans experiences for them, interacts with them, documents their development, and communicates with their families. I use the words classroom, learning environment, environment, and setting interchangeably as well.

When using the term family or families, I am referring to parents, grandparents, guardians, caregivers, or anyone who cares for the child and is responsible for them. There is one section in Chapter 7 that does address parents specifically (although this may still refer to anyone caring for the child), otherwise, the word family is used.

When referring to letters and sounds, individual letters are written in their capital form and sounds are denoted by /_/. (Example: K, /k/)

INTRODUCTION

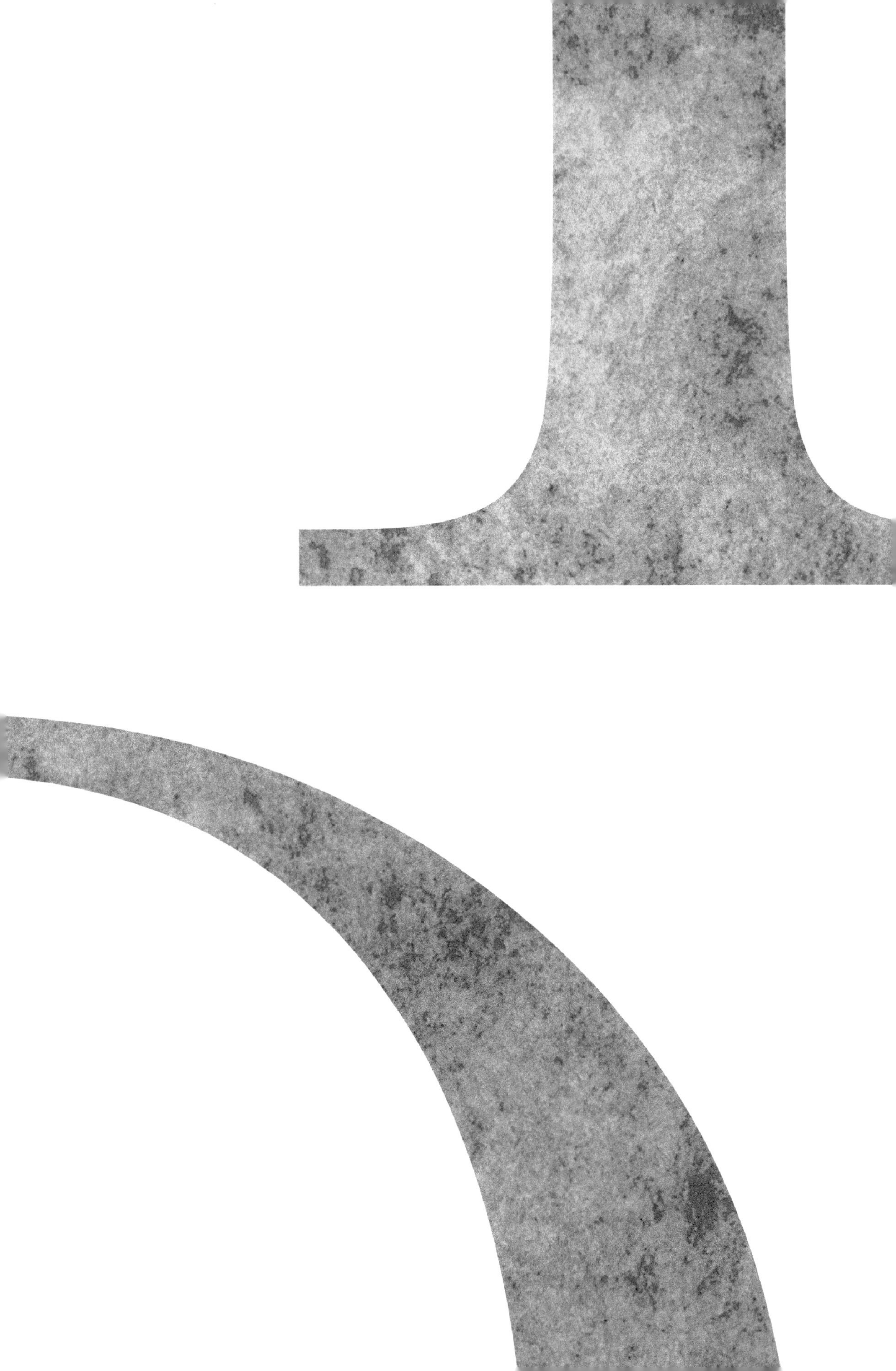

What is your favorite letter?

What is your favorite letter? Think about it. What does it look like? What does it sound like? What does it feel like when you say it? What is it about the letter that you love?

Let's consider that letter. Why is it your favorite? Is it the first letter of your name? Maybe it's the letter of a close family member or friend's name, or a letter you find unique. Whatever the connection, for some reason your favorite letter resonates with you. Children also have a favorite letter. It is usually the first letter of their first name because that's the letter they have seen and the sound they have heard their entire lives. It is the letter that identifies and signifies them. This is where alphabet knowledge begins, with the child and the child's world.

CHAPTER ONE

The Cornerstones of Language and Literacy

Everything has a starting point when it comes to child development and learning. This includes the ability to read and write. Before diving into alphabet knowledge, let's explore and dig into the roots of language and literacy.

The Whole Child

"A young child's brain is concerned with developing the whole child – not just the future student" (Connell & McCarthy, 2014).

Literacy begins with embracing the whole child, not introducing reading and writing instruction at an early age. Instead of fixating on outcomes, we need to focus on building strong foundations. For this to be possible, it is necessary to understand and respect the stages of child development.

Child Development

Comprehending child development consists of recognizing the different domains (cognitive, social/ emotional, language, and physical) and appreciating that they are interdependent and work together to create the whole child. But truly understanding the intricacies of child development goes deeper than just identifying those domains. It is grasping how every domain has developmental stages that build upon one another and create foundations for children to function and thrive in the world. Acknowledging that all children move through basically the same stages, albeit at different, individual rates, is also crucial. Knowing there are various stages is not enough, we need to be able to identify them and articulate why each one is important. Having this information helps us design environments and experiences that meet the developmental needs of young children. We do children a disservice when we ignore child development and insist on instruction that is beyond their developmental capabilities.

Developmental milestones

When looking at developmental milestones, it is important to recognize that although there typically is a consistent and predictable pattern of development, each child is unique and has their own, individual timeframe for progressing through each stage. This is why "ages and stages" need to be recognized as approximations and average guidelines, not benchmarks set in stone.

It is also important to remember that with new research, our profession is learning more and more about child development. As new information emerges, it may shift the approximations that make developmental milestones.

The Brain

Understanding how the brain develops is a critical component in overall child development along with language and literacy. Speaking in layperson's terms, here are two statements you will hear often throughout this book:

> Interactive experiences make connections and wire the brain. Repetition of those experiences strengthens that wiring.

> Children are very intuitive. Their brains tell them what they need to develop and their bodies respond appropriately. Therefore, we should always be observing children and following their cues because their actions tell us exactly what they need for development and learning.

Knowing this reinforces the fact that authentic, child-led play is vital to development. Plainly said, without play, children's brains cannot develop fully. What more effective way for children to have interactive experiences, than through play? How better to let them respond to what their brains are telling them they need, than by creating an environment that encourages them to lead their play? And when it comes to designing a space that is conducive to repeating actions as needed, what beats child-led play? The answer is nothing. Absolutely nothing is better than child-led play when it comes to a child's development.

CHAPTER ONE

Let's talk repetition

True repetition is when children repeat something again and again on their own accord to their level of satisfaction, not the adult's. When the adult requires children to do something time and again (such as doing the same group time activity everyday), that falls into the "drill" category and is not the same as child-led repetition. (It is also not child-centered.) If a child is repeating an action or a play scenario, there is a reason, there is a need for it. Maybe they are trying to figure something out. It might be they want to improve upon something. Or perhaps they just truly enjoy the experience. Whatever it may be, we need to trust that children are following their instincts, and create an environment that encourages that. Which brings us back to child-led play, the best opportunity for repetition to occur. Figure 1 is a comparison chart of child-led repetition versus adult "drill" activities.

Figure 1

Child-led repetition	Adult "drill" activities
Children ask for the same book to be read multiple times at group time for several days in a row.	Adult does the same thing at every group time including calendar, weather chart, and singing the same songs.
Children singing the same song with fun sounds in it repeatedly during outside play.	Adult goes through alphabet cards every day asking what sounds the letters make.
Child draws the same picture every day for a week, slightly changing it each time, placing the first letter of their name at the top.	Adult has children do traceable worksheets every day for the letter of the week.

Everything Starts Somewhere

When do language and literacy begin? Whether we are looking at overall child development or "desired academic outcomes," my catch phrase is "everything starts somewhere." The starting point for language and literacy is the moment a child is born. As soon as a newborn is placed in our arms, we make eye contact and start engaging with them. We have conversations and interact with them throughout the day as time goes on. It is during these moments that their brains start making connections to hear and produce language. (Experiences wire the brain; repetition strengthens the wiring.) Since language is the core of literacy, this is where it all begins. Not from early curriculum instruction, but through authentic interactions and experiences that support development.

Early Literacy Fundamentals

"We have to look at the whole child, not just some widget in him that is labeled 'reading readiness'" (Christakis, 2016).

Years ago, I created this chart (Figure 2) to give a snapshot of the fundamentals needed for language and literacy. Many of the skills could go in multiple categories and the majority could be dissected into even more intricate details. The goal is to give an overall view of the numerous foundations needed to support literacy.

Figure 2 - Early Literacy Fundamentals*

EARLY LITERACY

LANGUAGE

- Receptive
  - Auditory Sense
  - Phonological Awareness
  - Cognitive
- Expressive
  - Cognitive
  - Articulation/Vocabulary
  - Social/Emotional
  - Alphabet Knowledge
  - Visual Processing
  - Phonological Awareness

LITERACY

- Reading
  - Decoding
    - Language
    - Print Concepts
    - Print Awareness
    - Print Conventions
  - Comprehension
    - Language
    - Reasoning/Memory Recall
    - Background Knowledge
- Writing
  - Composition
    - Language
    - Experiences
    - Social/Emotional
  - Motor
    - Gross/Fine
    - Eye-Body
    - Senses

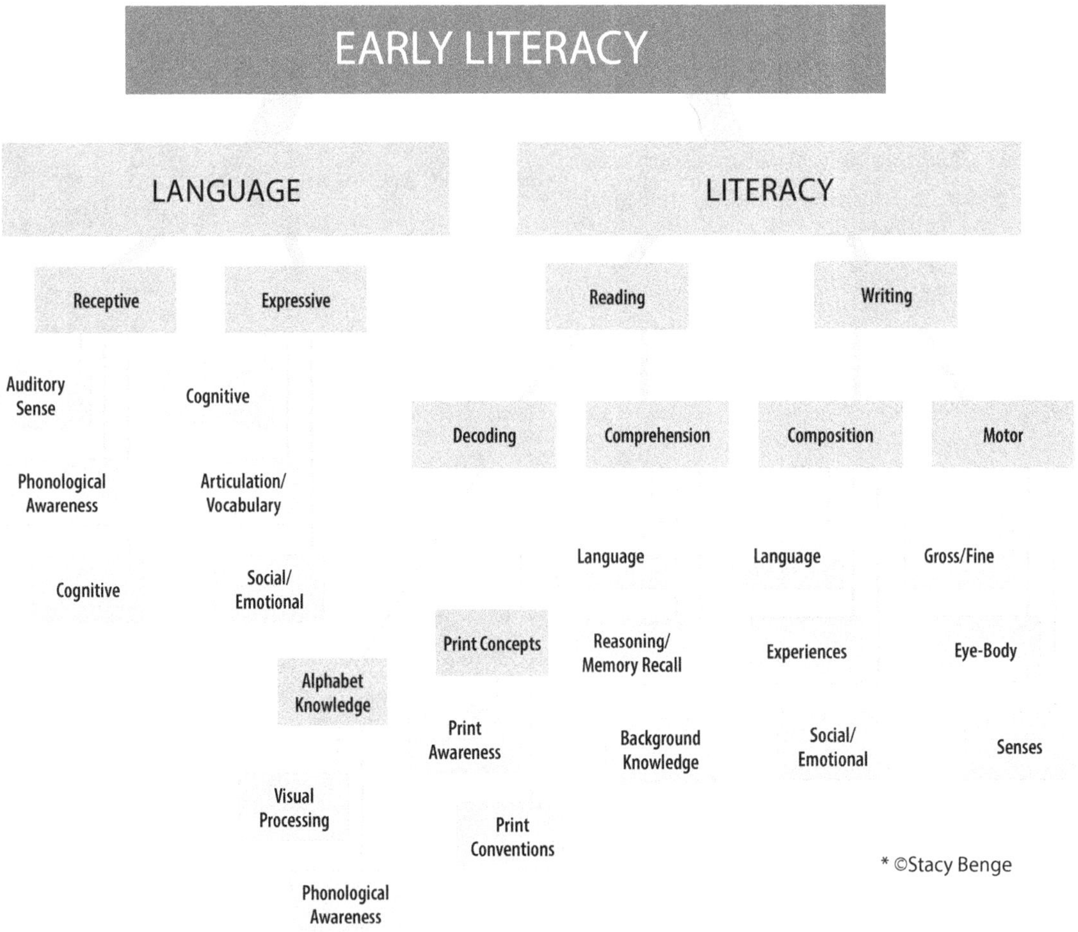

*©Stacy Benge

Let's break this chart down to see what is needed for children to eventually read and write. As we walk through, keep in mind that all these components are necessary, but not sufficient on their own. In other words, none of them work in isolation; they are interconnected to support literacy. This is why it is crucial to recognize the whole child when it comes to reading and writing.

Language

"When children have problems acquiring language, they are at high risk for difficulty in learning to read and write, and to listen and speak" (Spracher, 2000).

The core of literacy is language development; without it, children will not be competent readers and writers. How do children develop their language skills? By using them! All the time, and in a meaningful context. Therefore, a quiet classroom does not develop language. An environment where children's conversations center around scripted prompts or questions provided by a curriculum doesn't cut it either. The optimal way for children to develop language is through child-led play where they can utilize and build their skills by talking and having conversations in a natural setting.

Language development requires both receptive and expressive language. Let's look at what those entail.

Receptive Language

Receptive language is understanding and comprehending messages received through verbal and nonverbal means. From a verbal standpoint, receptive language depends on the auditory sense, phonological awareness, and cognitive processing. The auditory sense is more than just hearing; it is listening and maintaining attention to language being spoken. "Listening is a whole-brain, whole body experience that connects us to our environment and is the precursor to interaction, speaking, reading, and writing" (Hanscom, 2016). The brain also needs the ability to decipher and process the sound structures of language while listening; this is phonological awareness. Once the message makes its way to the brain, the cognitive skills kick in to process and understand it. The mind then retains the information and stores it to possibly be recalled later.

Expressive Language

Expressive language is communicating thoughts through spoken or written words as well as body and facial expressions. Cognitive processing enables a person to comprise that message, put it together in words, and then say it out loud or write it. Verbal expression specifically requires articulation which is the motor aspect of language. Articulation is a person's ability to pull air from the lungs and use the vocal cords, teeth, tongue, lips, and really, the entire mouth, to produce and combine sounds to create words. Generating those words also requires vocabulary knowledge. Expressive language has a social and emotional side as well, which includes engaging in a reciprocal conversation with another person.

Literacy

Language development is essential for literacy, but other fundamentals are required, too. The following gives a snapshot of foundational skills needed to support reading and writing.

Reading

Reading can generally be divided into two categories: decoding and comprehension. These two mechanisms work together to build competent readers.

Decoding

Decoding is the process of translating letters into sounds and either blending them together or segmenting them apart to read or write words. This requires alphabet knowledge and understanding the relationship between letters and sounds. Decoding also requires concepts related to print. Print awareness is recognizing that print is symbolic and carries meaning. Knowing print conventions, such as the direction of reading and writing going from left to right and top to bottom, is also important.

Comprehension

We learn to read, then we read to learn. Comprehension is understanding what has been read. Language development is critical for this process. Reasoning skills and memory recall also play a part in comprehension, allowing a reader to gain knowledge and retain it for later use. Background knowledge is also important to give context to the content being read. "Young children use background knowledge to comprehend books they hear read aloud…" (Schickedanz & Collins, 2013). If you are wondering how young children learn about the world and gain background knowledge, the answer is through child-led play!

Writing

In addition to reading there is the writing element of literacy, which consists of creating a message and physically writing it by hand. Together, these two components enable a person to communicate in written form.

Writing composition

Writing composition is generating a message to share with others, for the purpose of conveying information or telling a story. Before creating the message, a person must have the ability to form and compose the words from a language standpoint, making language development essential for this process. Deciding what to share often comes from a person's life and experiences. Having the desire to share and knowing the appropriate time to do so, hinges on social and emotional development.

Motor skills

The motor aspect of writing enables a person to hold a writing utensil in their hand, then draw and write. Handwriting requires more than fine motor skills; it is a full body experience as gross motor strength supports small muscle movements. The eye-body coordination allows the eyes and hands to work as a team and maneuver the pencil about the paper while writing. The vestibular and proprioceptive systems (the internal senses) exist to keep the body steady and inform it on how much strength is needed to hold the pencil and how much pressure to use when placing it on the paper.

What is Alphabet Knowledge?

"What letter is that?" Do you ever find yourself asking children this question? Both the educational and mainstream worlds tend to latch on to children naming the letters. Think of all the toys, children's books, curriculums, and apps that revolve around teaching the alphabet. We have put forth extensive effort when it comes to encouraging children learning their letters.

Do children need to learn the alphabet? Absolutely. It is a vital part of literacy. However, it is only a small piece of the puzzle, which is an in-depth process that requires more than just naming the letters. True alphabet knowledge is multifaceted and requires development of the whole child. To better understand this, let's look at what all it entails.

Letters Exist and Serve a Purpose

"For kids, 'Apple is for A' is what makes sense. It starts with the known (Apple) and relates it to the unknown (A). It moves from the tangible to the intangible, from the concrete to the symbolic" (Connell & McCarthy, 2014).

Before children can learn the alphabet, they must make the connection that letters exist and serve a purpose in reading and writing. This requires print awareness, which is knowing that letters are more than mere squiggles, but rather symbols that carry meaning. (A concept that hinges on the child being able to think abstractly and symbolically.) Until children develop this, alphabet instruction is useless.

Every Letter has a Distinct Appearance

Part of alphabet knowledge is understanding that every letter has a unique appearance in the upper- and lower-case formats and will always look that way. Regardless of what font the letter A is written in, it will consistently be the letter A, no matter what. I refer to this as the visual component of alphabet knowledge, as it requires visual perception to decipher and identify the unique shapes of the letters.

Every Letter has a Unique Sound

There's also an auditory component to alphabet knowledge. This is knowing that when we see a letter, it represents a distinct and unique sound every time. Although a couple of letters might change based on the rules of phonics or represent a different sound when blended with other letters, overall, each letter sound is unique to itself. Processing these sounds requires phonological awareness (particularly phonemic awareness) as well as the auditory sense.

Relationship Between Letters and Sounds

Alphabet knowledge culminates with understanding the relationship between the appearance of the letter and the sound it makes. When I see a letter, not only can I name it, but I know it represents a distinct sound. When I combine a letter with other letters, I can create a combination of sounds that make words. When I read words, the letters work together to signify what sounds to make. When I want to write, I use letters to represent the sounds of the words I want to create. Regardless of the context in which the alphabet is being used, the visual and auditory components always go hand in hand.

CHAPTER ONE

The Starting Point for Alphabet Knowledge

As mentioned previously, alphabet knowledge is a small but important component of literacy. It is necessary, but not sufficient on its own. Alphabet knowledge must work in conjunction with other developmental skills for reading and writing. This is why focusing on the whole child is so important. Knowing this should influence how literacy is approached in the classroom. When looking at alphabet knowledge specifically, it is essential to respect the foundational skills that need to be developed and create an environment that supports the growth of those skills. The following fundamentals need to be present for children to learn the letters:

- Interest and connection to letters and understanding that they serve a purpose

- Visual perception to recognize the distinct shape and appearance of letters

- Phonological awareness to hear the sounds of language and the letters

- Physical development to support handwriting for writing letters

The concept of alphabet knowledge needs to go beyond just naming letters and their sounds. The mindset should embrace the foundational skills and recognize that if the experience develops foundational skills, it is supporting alphabet knowledge, even if it isn't an "alphabet based" activity. This completely transforms the outlook of the learning environment, and brings to light how crucial child-led play is in this process. Move past the lesson plans dictated by purchased curriculums that focus on a preset list of outcomes. Leave behind activities that revolve around letter of the week, flash cards, and worksheets, as these tend to skip steps and just "surface teach." Instead, seek child-centered approaches that acknowledge the solid foundations necessary for alphabet knowledge. Create environments and experiences that respect the whole child and encourage children to play and develop the fundamentals needed for literacy.

Figure 3

ALPHABET KNOWLEDGE

| Interest and connection to letters | Phonemic awareness for letter sounds | Visual processing for letter recognition | Physical development for letter writing |

Understanding the Existence and Purpose of Letters

Please note, the remainder of the book assumes that children understand that letters exist and serve a purpose. This doesn't mean they know every letter but instead, they comprehend the symbolic significance of the alphabet in written language. How will you know when this starts to emerge? The children will tell you. Not directly, but through their actions. Letters will start to appear on their drawings. They will let you know when they see the first letter of their name, or one of their family members, somewhere in the environment. Children might even ask you about certain letters. The important thing to notice is that the children are guiding the conversation about the alphabet, not you. If so, it is probably a good indicator that they are beginning to understand that letters are meaningful and more than just mere squiggles in the world.

How can adults promote this? Introducing the alphabet at an early age does not jump-start this process. Children need to develop symbolic reasoning first, and child-led play is the best way for that to happen. It is also a good idea to demonstrate using letters in a meaningful context. Find natural opportunities to write in front of children such as writing their names, writing words they ask you how to spell, or transcribing stories they have created. Verbally say the letters as you write them. When reading, move your finger along the text so they can see you decode the letters to form words. I call these interactions being spontaneously intentional. They are not planned, but you are ready and available for them when they organically occur.

CHAPTER ONE

CHAPTER TWO

CHAPTER TWO

Learning the Alphabet Begins with Interest and Connection

When my youngest son, Jackson, was three years old, his preschool used the alphabet as the weekly theme. That was it, the theme was the letter of the week and all the activities in the room connected to that letter. Although the experiences were hands-on, my son had no interest in the alphabet. Jackson cared about race cars and trains and playing with anything connected to race cars and trains. Reading and writing were not on his radar. Can you guess the one and only letter Jackson knew at the end of the year? Jackson knew the letter J. That was it. It was his letter and it identified him, so of course, that was the one he knew. I think there was some frustration from his teacher, but I recognized that he was not ready for alphabet instruction.

Jackson's interest didn't increase much the following year. Before starting kindergarten, he knew J (for his name and my husband, Jason), S for my name, and M for my other son, Mason. Oh – and he knew B, for our last name. That was it! Again, I wasn't concerned. Jackson had great communication skills and an extensive vocabulary. He also functioned quite nicely in the classroom and got along well with his friends. I had no doubt he would thrive in kindergarten regardless of only knowing four letters.

Fast forward to kindergarten. My husband and I went for the beginning of the year conference with his teacher about a month after school started. Fully expecting to hear that Jackson didn't know any letters, we were surprised when his teacher told us he knew all his upper and lowercase letters with no hesitation or concern. What changed? Jackson's interest and motivation. Did he have the desire to be a better reader and writer? Kind of, but not exactly. Jackson's kindergarten teacher had become his biggest crush, and his mission became to get her to marry him. Yes – an ambitious goal for a five-year-old, but he wanted to do what he could to impress her. What was the best way to go about that? Showcase all his intelligence and knowledge. How could Ms. Walker not be wooed by Jackson knowing the entire alphabet, both upper and lower case? And therein lied Jackson's motivation. His desire to learn the alphabet had nothing to do with how the information was presented. It had nothing to do with the songs that were sung, or the items glued on the construction paper in the form of the letter. His motivation resided in gaining the attention of an important person in his life, someone he admired and adored.

Everything Starts Somewhere

Developing an interest and connection to the alphabet begins with the child and their world. It begins with what is important to them in the here and now. It doesn't depend on the alphabet curriculum chosen by the school. It is not a matter of what activities, songs, and crafts were completed. The child's motivation depends on what is applicable to their world, and what is important and relevant to them.

No More Letter of the Week

Let's look at letter of the week themes, a common practice in some early childhood programs. Before doing so, it is important to open the heart and mind and be ready to examine current thoughts and practices. Growth doesn't happen without challenge, right? And please know, if letter of the week is implemented in your setting, this is not to criticize, but to create an opportunity to reflect and consider a more effective way to approach alphabet knowledge. Part of professional growth is learning and refining pedagogy.

CHAPTER TWO

Why Letter of the Week?

Why do we do letter of the week? Why do we pick one letter and for the entire week, do everything for this letter? We sing songs about the letter, glue items on the letter, bring something from home starting with that letter, and play with puppets that have that letter on them. The following week, we repeat everything again for the next letter. The process continues until all the letters have been checked off. Why do we this?

Answers I have heard include: "We do it to make sure that we give equal, thorough instruction to all the letters, so the children truly learn them" and "Because our curriculum requires letter of the week activities" and "It's easier to plan. There is a system to it that makes it easy to check everything off and then we can repeat those plans year after year." But the most common response I hear is, "We have never really questioned it. It's just the way it's always been done." But is letter of the week instruction truly the best way for children to learn the alphabet?

Letter of the Week in Perspective

Let's play a game. Let's pretend that you are in my preschool class, and we are learning the letters. It is group time and I introduce our letter of the week. I show you this flash card and say,

"Do you know what letter this is? This is 'KEY'. Do you know what sound 'KEY' makes? It makes the /ksh/ sound. And guess what? This week, we are learning all about the letter 'KEY'. We are going to look at this flash card every day. We're going to glue cotton on the letter 'KEY'. You're going to bring pictures of objects that start with the letter 'KEY' for show and share. I am going to introduce the 'KEY' puppet and we're going to sing songs about the letter 'KEY' all week long. And I am going to ask you every day what in our school starts with the letter 'KEY'. Do you know why? Because 'KEY' is our letter of the week!"

We get to the following week. "Guess what our letter of the week is? It is 'PIN'."

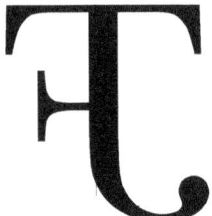

'PIN' makes the /peep/ sound. We're going to glue all the things on 'PIN' and sing songs about 'PIN'. You are going to bring pictures from home that start with 'PIN'. We will also play with the puppet that has the letter 'PIN' on it, because 'PIN' is our letter of the week." Another week of pretty much the same activities, but using a different letter.

And for weeks to come, the grown-ups at home are going to ask, "What sound does 'KEY' make?" and "What does 'PIN' look like?" You are probably going to be able to answer them that week and possibly the following week, based on the fact that you memorized these "letters" and for the time being, you can repeat them. And people will be impressed and think that you're ready for school and that you should be fast tracked to advanced reading. They're also going to give your teacher (me!) praise for being the best teacher around, for teaching all the children in the class all the letters!

Sounds great, right? Well, let's jump ahead a month or so. The opportunity arises to revisit the letters we "studied" in the weeks past. Are you going to remember 'KEY' and 'PIN'? Will you be able to tell me about their sounds off the top of your head? Will these letters make any sense to you? Probably not. Why? These letters bear no relevance to your life or your world. There is no context for you to connect to them. Your name doesn't start with 'KEY' or 'PIN.' You don't have any family members that start with those letters either. These are not letters you're going to see in your immediate environment on a daily basis. For the time being, there is no motivation for you to know these letters other than me introducing them to you as letter of the week, and that is not enough for you to remember them.

While 'KEY' and 'PIN' are made-up letters, this is what we do with young children when we introduce the alphabet in a prescribed letter of the week manner. The letter we're focusing on for that week does not connect to the child's world, so the child does not connect to that letter. This is "surface teaching" where there is no deep knowledge, just short-lived memorization. For children to learn the alphabet, they must have an interest and connection to the letters and the letters must associate with their world. This is the reason that letter of the week is not the most effective way to introduce the alphabet, yet many of our programs and curriculums follow this approach.

Child-Centered Alphabet Approach

Like everything else in our settings, approaching the alphabet should be child-centered. This requires building relationships with each child in our care and getting to know them on a personal basis. "[Researcher Urie] Bronfenbrenner proposed that children's experiences in the social world in which they lived and grew were highly significant in their learning and development" (Neaum, 2017). Every child has an "ecosystem" that is unique and individual to them. What is the center of that ecosystem? The child, because they are the center of their world! The next layer is their family including their parents, siblings, pets, and whomever is part of their home environment. The outer ring is their friends, including school friends, neighbors, or peers from extracurricular activities. Since all children come from different backgrounds, their ecosystem is going to be specific to them. Paying attention to the child's ecosystem enables us to learn about their lives and interests and connect to their world.

Figure 4 - Center of their World

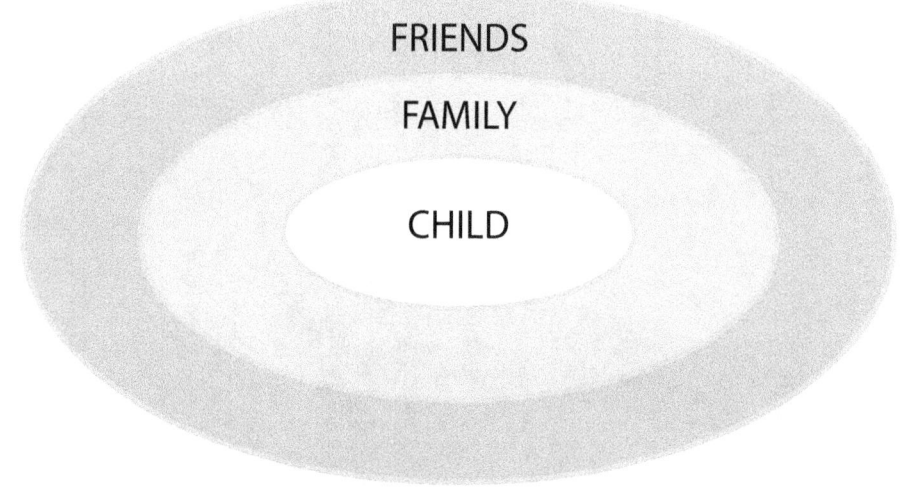

If what is happening in the classroom does not connect to the child, then the child will not connect to it. This pertains to everything within the setting, not just alphabet knowledge. The environments, the experiences, and our interactions all have to connect to the child, in order to resonate with them. Consider this, at the beginning of the school year, how can we plan ahead when we don't even know the children yet? Better yet, how can a curriculum company that has never entered our learning environment create a year's worth of lesson plans when they don't know us or our group of children? Each individual child's ecosystem needs to be considered, and that can only be done once we build relationships with the children. Alphabet knowledge is best approached in the same way.

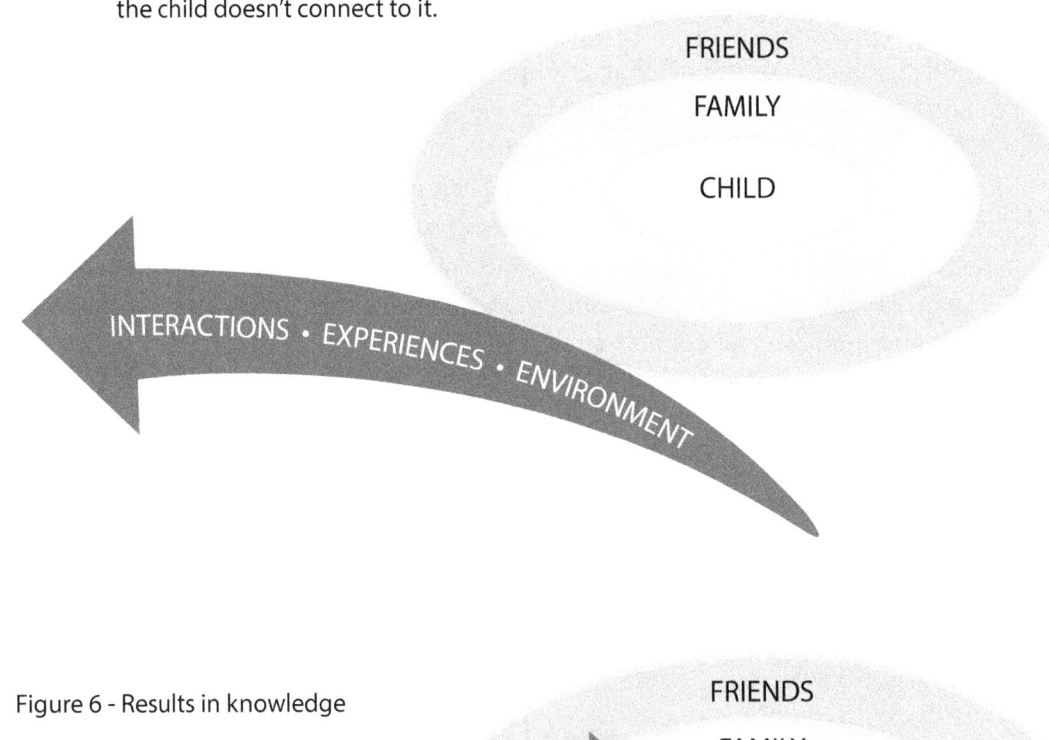

Figure 5 - If it doesn't connect to the child, the child doesn't connect to it.

Figure 6 - Results in knowledge

Everything in the classroom must connect to the child's world and ecosystem. When the environment, experiences, and interactions connect to the child, they learn, and this results in true knowledge. Alphabet experiences (and everything else) must respect what is important to the individual children presently in the class. If they have an interest or a connection to the letters, and the letters are meaningful in their worlds, children will learn the letters, bond with them, and retain them because the letters serve a purpose in children's lives.

Alternatives to Letter of the Week

If there is no letter of the week, how do we teach the alphabet? "[Data and research] indicate that, when it comes to classroom practice, (1) not every letter requires the same instructional attention; (2) whole-class instruction focused on a particular letter is inefficient…; (3) no one sequence for teaching letters and their associated sounds is optimal for all children" (McKay & Teale, 2015). This is wonderful news because it frees us from the constraints of only one letter at a time.

Knowing this empowers us to introduce the alphabet in an organic manner that is meaningful to children. But how is that done? It starts with adults modeling reading and writing in everyday life. During group times, read books and write out messages. In addition to paper and crayons, have books available throughout the entire environment, accessible for children's play. Be available to read and write at the child's request. Also, find opportunities for children to see you read and write for day-to-day routines such as writing names for attendance or reading a note from home. These naturally-occurring encounters are perfect opportunities for children to experience and learn the letters. While they may seem simple and might not fall under the category of "instruction," they are a powerful and effective way to teach the alphabet.

What if I am required to designate "target" letters?

What if you are required to select focus letters for planning purposes? A holistic and spiral approach is a great place to start. Instead of one letter a week, maybe focus on two, three, five, or even eight at at time. There is no limit or rule on the amount of letters to expose children to at once. "[Research has not] found any advantage to exposing preschoolers to just one or two letters at a time... If children's exposure is restricted to one letter a week, or even two or three, opportunities to compare and contrast letters are reduced" (Schickedanz & Collins, 2013). How will you know how many letters to highlight? Get to know your children, observe them, and read their cues. If the letters are relevant to the children's world, they can learn more than one letter at a time. Keep in mind, with a spiral approach, there is an ebb and flow with the focus changing, or staying the same, based on the children's interests. The point of the spiral is to revisit the letters several times throughout the school year as well as provide abundant opportunities to interact with letters in a meaningful context.

What letters do I pick first?

Start with letters children show an interest in. Let's go back to when I asked you about your favorite letter at the beginning of the book. What letter did you pick? Was it the first letter of your first name? Was it the letter of a family member or significant other? Was it a letter that you just always liked or found unique for some reason? Whatever it may be, your favorite letter is important because it connects to you in some form or fashion, even if randomly picked. When you get to know the children presently in your class, you will learn their favorite letters and that should be your guide.

The first letters of the children's first names are a great place to start. "While researchers have not yet found a best order for teaching alphabet letters, there is an 'own-name advantage,' meaning that a child usually learns the first letter in her own name (and in the names of family members) before learning other letters" (Schickedanz & Collins, 2018). The first name letters are what children have seen and heard their entire lives; start with those and go from there. Again, there's no limit to how many letters to introduce at one time. Just read the cues of the children and always ask if what you are doing is connecting with them.

How exactly does this work? Let's say I have children in my class named: Ashlin, Brenda, Danny, Emily, Finley, Graham, Greg, Jackson, Jason, Kris, Mason, Matt, and Megan. Then, you have my name as the teacher, Stacy, because I am part of the class too. These are the letters to start with: A, B, D, E, F, G, J, K, M and S.

Figure 7 - Holistic Letter Approach

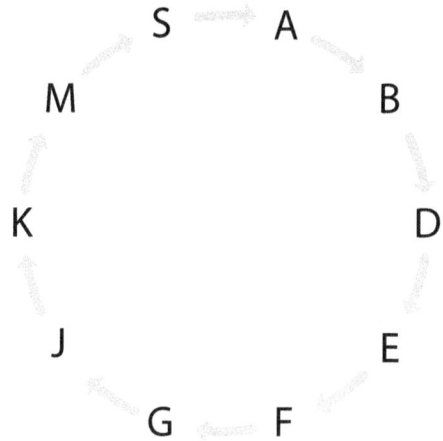

Wow! That is 10 letters! Don't let this be overwhelming. Just because these are the selected letters doesn't mean planning activities for every child to do for every letter. Instead, it is making sure these letters are introduced and represented in a meaningful context within the setting. This allows each child to have interactions with their first name letter in a way that uniquely connects to them.

What does this look like in the classroom? Begin by providing materials that relate to the selected letters throughout the environment amongst other toys and resources. Have some possible group time experiences planned and ready to go if the children seem interested. Perhaps include some activities to be used during transition times that pertain to these letters. The point is to provide possible opportunities for children to interact with the selected letters in a way that connects to them. (Details on these ideas will be explored in the next section.)

After some observation, you may notice it is time to introduce some new letters. At this point, go back to the ecosystems. What is important to the children at the present time? What are the family member's names? What play scenarios are being acted out? Any other new interests in the children's lives? What do we overhear them discussing when they are playing? Whatever is happening should guide the next move.

Let's say that Mason has a new sibling named Thomas. The letter T just became important to him. We have been reading the book *No, David!* by David Shannon quite a bit. You notice the children are always acting out the book and saying, "No David!" You have also been asked several times to write "No David!"

when the they are playing. Could this make the letter N a contender? The children also keep asking to sing Willaby Wallaby Woo. Can we utilize that to introduce the letter W? All of these observations might be enough evidence to spiral in the next layer of letters (T, N, and W) into the mix. Make the decision and go from there.

Figure 8 - Holistic Letter Approach

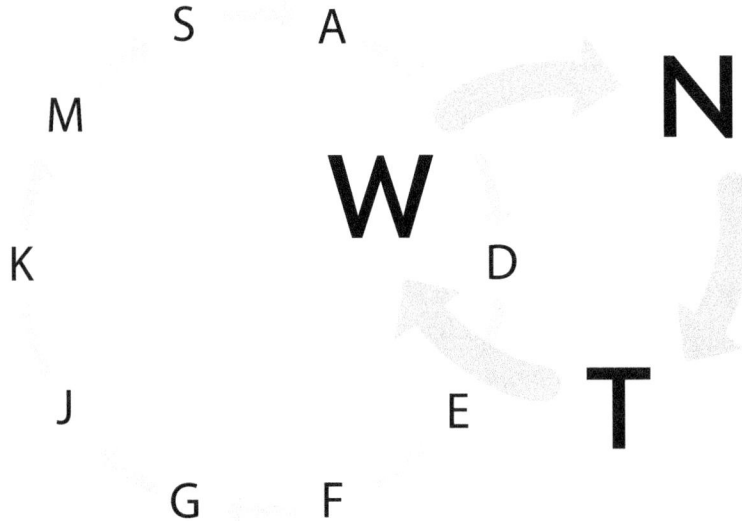

This is not a one stop shop. Revisit these letters as many times as needed at any time throughout the school year, as the opportunity arises! Introduce and explore the letters as the interest emerges. It is a completely different mindset, but it is liberating and so much more effective than sticking to the prescribed one letter at a time approach.

Why is this information important?

Knowing the foundational skills needed to support alphabet knowledge and overall literacy helps define our pedagogy. Understanding what research indicates are optimal practices for children learning their letters helps shape what we do in our settings. This knowledge also helps us defend against ineffective instruction, such as letter of the week, and advocate for child-centered experiences revolving around play. Having this information supports our conversations with stakeholders as we explain our approaches to alphabet knowledge in our learning environments.

CHAPTER TWO

Experiences To Promote an Interest in Letters and Connection to Them

Think beyond teacher instruction when it comes to alphabet knowledge. Consider it like having the letters in the back of your mind, placing them naturally in the environment, and being ready to address them in a meaningful context. Children need to have experiences with the letters in ways that connect to their worlds. And remember the foundational skills mentioned earlier? If an experience relates to those, although not "letter-based," it still supports alphabet knowledge. This occurs naturally when children are playing. Let's look at how this happens in our settings.

Seize the Opportunity, Without Interruption

Recently, my three-year-old niece came over and we played with a pretend pig playset. As we were playing, my niece started to say, "It is a pretend pig, purple pancake picnic!" We started laughing because it sounded so funny, and we said this over and over and over again. My "teacher self" began to creep in and I started to feel the need to make this a "teachable moment." I couldn't resist, and I said, "Pretend pig, purple pancake picnic. Do you know what letter all those words start with?" I remember my niece looking at me with an expression that said, "That's not the game we're playing Stacy!" I realized in that moment that I overstepped and interrupted a fun play experience we were having, by trying to teach a letter. I quickly shifted back into play mode and said, "Pretend pig, purple pancake picnic!" while laughing along. Later, it occurred to me that alphabet knowledge was actually happening because my niece was hearing the /p/ sound repeatedly. I didn't need to identify at that moment that it was connected to the letter P. She was hearing those sounds in a playful and meaningful context, and developing phonemic awareness. The moral of the story? Respect the experience for what it is and don't sacrifice learning for the sake of a teachable moment during play.

So, with that in mind, find natural opportunities to have conversations, sing, read, and write with children and see if that yields the chance to experience letters in a natural context, not just at a designated time. If children have developed an interest in the alphabet, these experiences will happen organically. They will ask about letters and bring them into the conversation. Follow the cues and don't hijack the experience with a lesson on the letter.

Write in the Presence of Children

Seek opportunities to write in front of children. This can be planned or spontaneous. It is even better when it is requested by the child and connects to their play. Verbally spell the words while writing, too. The idea is for children to see you use letters to write, compose and communicate messages.

Materials in the Environment

Place materials that pertain to the alphabet throughout the entire environment. This is not confined to the literacy center. Place books everywhere, and not just alphabet books; all books have letters in them creating words, so they all promote alphabet knowledge and literacy. Provide blank paper and crayons throughout the setting so children can draw and write if they choose. Letter stamps, letter blocks, magnetic letters, and wooden letters can also be used throughout various areas of the room. Place letter cutouts in the art center with an abundance of materials to decorate them if the children choose. Provide scissors and glue to cut the letters up for use in other art creations. The point is to integrate these materials throughout the classroom to be used during child-led play.

The materials could include the entire alphabet or perhaps just the letters being highlighted. Remember to observe. If you place something in the setting and it is not gaining any interest, try it in a different area of the room or remove it and bring it back later. If certain materials are popular and being played with every day, leave them there because they are serving a purpose; no need to remove them just because the lesson plan says to do so. The environment needs to evolve alongside the children's interests. Their actions will tell you when it is time to start moving on to something new. When this happens, rotate the materials, and replace them with something else.

Don't Saturate the Environment with the Alphabet

Keep in mind, the whole setting should not be inundated with alphabet materials, this should just be a small portion of what is happening in the classroom. Think of the letters as supporting cast members. They are there, they serve a purpose, but they are not the main focus. Keep in mind the fundamentals of alphabet knowledge. Designing an environment that supports child-led play will develop all those skills, so don't exhaust all efforts on just the alphabet. Remember, literacy and alphabet knowledge require developing the whole child.

Opportunities for Children to Experience and Write Names

Place the children's names strategically around the room. On their cubbies, coat hooks, and lunch box shelf. Also provide opportunities for them to write their names if they want. This can be done from a teacher-directed standpoint or within play. Include attendance charts when children arrive at school, lunch count, and class graphs. Be sure to respect children's ability when it comes to writing. Their best attempt might just be writing the first letter of their first name, and that is okay. If a child is hesitant, you can offer to help or possibly have a name card they can place, instead of writing it out.

Planning Without Letter of the Week

How can you plan without letter of the week? I am not going to sugarcoat it; planning is one of the hardest parts about not doing letter of the week. The lesson plans from last year won't work this year, because there is a completely different set of children. This year's plans won't work for next year because, again, there will be a completely different set of children. Yes, this requires more work on our part, but this is part of being child-centered. Our practices are for the children, not ourselves or the stakeholders. Therefore, the lesson plans need to reflect the needs and interests of the children we are currently serving in the here and now.

Lesson plans help prepare and give us ideas, but they should not dictate everything we do. Think of the plan as a living, breathing document. It should fluctuate and be flexible to meet the needs of the children in our care. Follow the children's cues and be in the moment. It is alright to abandon the plans if the situation calls for it. Don't lose heart if you plan something and it flops. It is also okay if you plan something that works wonderfully and the children ask to repeat it over, and over, and over again. If they request that, there is a reason. This is child-led repetition! Follow their lead as they know best what they need.

Alphabet Knowledge Framework

The following is a framework of a possible way to generate ideas when focusing on multiple letters at one time. I don't consider it an actual lesson plan, but more of a brainstorming tool to be used in conjunction with your current lesson plan. The following table shows three letters at once, but that doesn't mean the focus can only be on three letters at a time. You might notice it states "Weeks of/ Month of" at the top right. This is because there is no limit on the amount of time spent highlighting specific letters. Let the children guide you on how many letters to focus on and how long to spend on those letters. Don't limit the opportunities to just a week's timeframe. If you start with the first name letters of the class, you might notice they are enjoying the experiences with their letters and their newfound friends' letters. If so, there is no need to rush to the rest of the alphabet. Simply let the children lavish in that space.

This guideline can be morphed into a variety of ways that work for you. The hope is it helps with designing an environment that supports multiple letters at once and brings about new ideas.

Before we break this down, remember this is not a lesson plan but a framework to help shift away from letter of the week. Comprehensive lesson plans should not solely focus on alphabet knowledge but rather the whole child. They should be all-encompassing and assist in designing a learning environment that supports all domains of child development and promotes child-led play.

Selecting the Letters
Observe children to see what letters might be important in their worlds. Continuing with the previous example, the decision has been made to spiral in T, N, and W. Once those are selected, go from there.

Possible Group Times
Follow the children's lead as you navigate the timing of introducing new letters at group time. You might have thought it a great idea to highlight the letter W but find that the class is not latching on. That is okay. Scrap the ideas and move to something else. What if the group time experience you designed spawns wonderful and amazing experiences that take you down a path you didn't expect? Don't miss that opportunity, follow that lead and go there! As long as what is being done is developmentally appropriate and respects the whole child, everything will be fine. Also, these group time ideas are not to be crammed into one day. They are possibilities to consider over an extended amount of time, and can be repeated at the children's request.

Figure 9

Ideas for Possible Alphabet Experiences

Lesson plan considerations		Weeks of/ Month of:
Letter T	**Letter N**	**Letter W**
Inspiration: Mason's new sibling named Thomas	Inspiration: Reading *No David!* Children ask how to spell "No"	Inspiration: Children continually request to sing Willaby Wallaby
Possible group time	Possible group time	Possible group time
• Show picture of baby Thomas • Compare /t/ and /d/ sounds • Play the letter clue game	• Have children say, "No David!" while reading along • Hold nose for /n/ sound	• Discuss how mouth feels when making /w/ sound • Substitute /w/ with other letter sounds while singing
Materials to add to environment		Possible activities
• Pictures of Thomas with name on them • Mirrors to see faces when talking • Cutouts of T, N, and W in art area • *No David!* Books around environment		• Tape selected letters on floor to walk and hop • Make first name letters with playdough • Thomas nonsense rhymes at transition
Reflection		Looking ahead
• Notice children pretending to be a dog named Lee • Brenda's mom getting married. Many conversations about mom's new last name changing to Kirkpatrick.		• What letters not introduced yet? • Introduce L • Revisit K

Here are some possible group time experiences. (Please note, these are discussed further in Chapters 3, 4, and 5.)

Letter T
Since the inspiration for the letter T is Mason's new sibling Thomas, let's ask his family to bring pictures of the new baby. We might pretend we are holding and rocking babies and discuss what songs we might sing. Play the letter clue game starting with T continuing it on with other letters. Let's say the name Thomas and place our hands on our necks and in front of our mouths to explore the initial /t/ sound. This might lead to comparing the /t/ and /d/ sounds and paying attention to how the mouth feels similar for both, since they are made the same, but one is voiced and the other is voiceless.

Letter N
By the children's request, we are continuously reading *No, David!* By David Shannon. There is a need there, so we will continue to read it. If it can be done in a natural context and not interrupt the flow of the story, point out the letter N in the title and possibly throughout the book. While reading, when we get to the parts where the mom says, "No, David!", we can all stand up and say it along with the story. What happens when we hold our noses and say, "No David!"? Let's try it and find out!

Letter W
We will keep singing "Willaby Wallaby," a class favorite. Let's put our hands around our mouths and talk about how it feels when we make the /w/ sound. Provide some mirrors to see what it looks like when making the /w/ sound. We might also substitute the /w/ sound in the song with other letter sounds children choose to use.

Materials in the Environment

A setting that encourages child-led play provides open-ended resources throughout the room, in every interest area, for children to use freely. The majority of these materials support alphabet knowledge in some form (whether they directly relate to the letters or not) because they connect to the foundational skills needed. Here are some ideas of materials that directly pertain to the letters mentioned earlier, that might be a good addition to the learning environment. The idea is for the children to have free access to the materials to use however they want. We don't have specific activities for these, they are just available to assist in the play. Keep in mind, these are not the only resources in the environment, but rather, supplements to all of the many other materials available.

- **Pictures of Thomas with name written by them**
  Since the inspiration for the letter T is a new sibling named Thomas, place pictures of the baby with the name on them throughout the setting. (Of course you would get the family's permission first.) This gives children the opportunity to see print in a meaningful context, but it might also inspire children to talk about their family members' names and how to spell them. If so, invite children to bring pictures of their siblings, family members, and friends which will spark writing those names too. If permission is given, post those pictures around the room as well.

- **Mirrors to see faces when talking**
  A powerful tool in learning to articulate sounds is actually seeing them being made. Since several of the group time experiences involve examining how the mouth feels when creating sounds, provide mirrors around the environment for children to see themselves talking. This could be handheld mirrors in various interest areas or placing mirrors on the wall.

- **Cutouts of T, N, and W in art area**
  These can be made with construction paper, cardboard, or even fabric. Children can decorate them if they want, but they could also cut them up and use them for other art inspirations. Maybe they want to take them to the block area to tape to block structures to represent signs. They might also find a use for them in the dramatic play area for a reason we never anticipated!

- ***No David!* Books around environment**
  Since these books are being read often at the children's request, place them around the classroom. Put some in a basket and take them outside. These are not the only books provided, but since they are popular, they definitely need to be available for the children to read.

Possible Activities

While I am not a fan of sitting an entire group of children down at the table to do the same activity, I recognize there is a time and place for adult-directed activities. They can be useful, as long as they do not impede on child-led play time, and don't overrun the daily schedule. My viewpoint is, for every minute spent with an adult guiding an activity, children should be equally repaid with child-led play time. Teacher-led activities need to be developmentally appropriate, engaging and hands-on, of the children's interest, and should not last longer than the collective group's attention to the activity. In other words, if half of the children have lost interest, move on to something else. Requiring a child to do something they don't want to do is not effective. Children have the right to choose whether or not to participate.

As we venture into the "possible activities," bear in mind, these are intended to be something you might do during a transition time when you have ten minutes to fill, or during a group time experience such as music and movement. You may even provide these experiences as options during play time. Don't think of these activities as something all the children have to do at one time.

- **Tape Letters on the Floor**
  For all the highlighted letters, tape their shapes on the floor for the children to walk, crawl, or jump around on, to see how to form them. Think big body on this. Maybe this stays on the floor for a while to be used at various times throughout the day. What if a child requests a specific letter on the floor? Find a way to do it. There is a reason the child asked, so take advantage of that!

- **Playdough Letters**
  We might have an experience where everybody makes their first name letters with playdough; therefore, not everyone is doing the same letter. If children are showing an interest in the activity, ask if there are other letters they would like to make. Let them choose what letters they want to create.

- **Nonsense Rhymes**
  For transitions, create nonsense rhymes for the name Thomas. This can be done while lining up or while transitioning to mealtimes. The children might start to ask to create nonsense rhymes for their own names or family member's names. That is great! Follow that cue and capitalize on their interest.

Reflection and Looking Ahead

It is important to reflect at the end of every day, week, or month for a variety of reasons. I constantly reflected on my lesson plans and wrote on them what did or did not work; that way, if I ever referred back to them, I had "in the moment" notes of things I would do the same or differently.

"When we plan as teacher researchers, we stay humble and curious, flexible and non-attached. We plan only one next offering, not weeks down the road, because we know that how the children make use of each offering will shape our next offering" (Pelo & Carter, 2018). It is important to reflect on what was observed from the children, to help guide the next steps.

Here are some examples of possible observations:

I've noticed that children are always pretending to be a dog named Lee. Not sure why? Maybe they've seen a movie, or somebody now has a dog named Lee? Whatever the reason may be, it is significant in their world, and this might be a chance to introduce the letter L. Maybe I offer to write tags with the name Lee on them to inspire their play and ensure the children watch me write out the letters. Perhaps I use the blocks to create a maze in the shape of an L that might be used for a transition. Before lining up, I write the name Lee in front of them on chart paper. I tell them the block maze is in the shape of an L, the first letter of Lee's name. Each child can walk the L maze on their way to line up.

—

Brenda's mom is getting married and going to have the new last name Kirkpatrick. Since children play about what is important in their lives, I notice Brenda and several other children pretending to get married and saying that is their new last name. The letter K has become significant. We have focused on it previously, but let's revisit it. I might write Kirkpatrick on some cards and envelopes and place them in the dramatic play area. Maybe I will find songs to sing and books to read that emphasize the /k/ sound. I can intentionally try these things and see if the children show any interest, then follow their lead.

—

What letters have not been highlighted yet? Is there a reason those particular letters have not been important? Have I overlooked something? Is there a way I can inconspicuously present these letters and see if children respond? Am I continuing to observe, reflect, and use the children's interests to guide my next steps?

Small Groups During Play?

In order to maximize the benefits of free, child-led play time, children should not be pulled from their play time for a teacher-conducted small group activity. It is counterproductive. If children are guiding their own play, they are: building curiosity, hypothesizing, figuring things out, increasing their attention spans, and, most importantly, they are learning! It does not make sense to remove children from play for an activity we, the stakeholders, or the predetermined curriculum deem important. If a learning environment is intentionally designed with compelling materials and resources, but children are constantly being removed for small group instruction, the environment does not serve its purpose. This is a prime example of adults interrupting children's learning by trying to teach.

Playing Alongside Children

While I didn't pull children for small group time during play, I did place myself in the play environment, start playing, and see who would join me. I did this every so often and found many times children were curious and wanted to play beside me. By their own choice, not my insistence or requirement, they would come and ask me what I was doing. I would tell them and then ask if they wanted to play too. It was an open invitation and their free will on whether or not to join. If they chose to, this gave me the chance to interact with them in a playful setting. I still followed cues, still let the children's interest guide my interactions. This provided the opportunity to have meaningful conversations without interrupting the play. That was the goal, not to create a teachable moment.

For example, while the children were playing, I plopped myself in the literacy area and started to read a book. If a child chose to come over and read with me, they were welcome. If they asked me to read a different book, we read it. If they asked me to play something else, we did.

Many times, I would go to the art center and write the letter S on a piece of paper and start decorating it. Usually, the children would come to the table and ask me what I was doing. I told them and asked if they wanted to join. If they said yes, I would ask what letter they wanted to decorate, instead of assuming it would be their first letter. First, this opened conversations. Secondly, I found many times the children wanted to decorate the letter S because, as their teacher, I was important to them, so that made "my letter" significant to them as well. Whatever letter they chose was fine. This led to conversations about different ways to decorate the letters, which gave me ideas of various materials to place in the art area in the future.

If children wanted to sit by me and do something else, that was totally fine too. The purpose of this was not to take over the play or guide an activity; it was to give me the opportunity to play alongside them. I found when I did this, children were more apt to invite me into their play in the future. Again, another great way to have conversations and build relationships.

Questions about play interactions

What if I start playing and nobody chooses to join me?
No problem, just follow the children's cues. They are engrossed in what they are doing and that is great. Use the time to observe and listen to the children for future planning.

Should I do this every day?
My answer is no. This is something you might do once or twice a week or some weeks not at all. Use your professional judgement. Remember, free play is the child's world, and our role is that of spectator. This is our best opportunity to observe and document, so we don't want to rob ourselves of that chance.

> *What if I am required to do a small group time during free play?*
>
> This opens the opportunities for us to have authentic conversations about our practices with stakeholders. Pulling children from play for small group activities defeats the purpose. If we are intentional in designing our learning environments, including providing big chunks of time for play, children will learn no matter what they are playing or who they are playing with. Invite stakeholders into the environment to observe. Make the learning visible to them and help them see the vast benefits of child-led play for desired outcomes.

Why do these experiences work?

Doing away with letter of the week and standardized curriculums frees us up to follow what is important to children and their worlds. Combining that with child-led play, children are able to experience the alphabet in an organic manner that is meaningful to them and their ecosystems. This child-centered approach respects that fact that children don't need the same amount of time to learn each letter and that they are capable of learning more than one letter at a time. This focus allows the children's interest to guide our practice, not a prescribed agenda created by people who are not familiar with our settings.

WHOLE CHILD ALPHABET

CHAPTER THREE

Letter Recognition Begins with Vision

"Approximately 80 percent of all learning comes through the visual pathways" (Lazarus, 2020). My oldest son's first grade teacher called me one day and told me Mason was putting his head down when doing desk work and when she asked him to sit up, he would lean over on his hand and cover his left eye. I took him to a developmental optometrist who diagnosed him with convergence insufficiency, a disorder where the eyes don't move inward when looking at close objects. (More about that later.) My mission to figure out how to help Mason ignited my fascination with the visual system, and how it develops and impacts learning. I came to realize the importance of the vision sense and why early childhood professionals should consider its magnitude when focusing on the whole child. It is also vital when it comes to alphabet knowledge and letter recognition.

The Starting Point for Letter Recognition

Think of all the times children are asked to look and identify objects. We get very excited when they start to recognize and identify letters and words. Being able to do this requires more than just memorization; it requires the sense of sight. Without it, children cannot distinguish the unique markings that differentiate each letter. This goes deeper than just eyesight. Reading, writing, and alphabet knowledge depend on visual perception, the brain's ability to make sense of the information coming in through the eyes. The sense of sight is not fully established at birth but instead is a process that must be developed and refined like any other area of child development.

A couple of notes before walking through this section. There are several different industries and fields that take interest in our sense of sight. Opthalmologists, optometrists, pediatricians, and occupational therapists all address children and vision in their practice. Because of this, there are variations in terminologies and classifications of eyesight. I have pulled the information together to give an overall picture of vision. Here are some resources to dig deeper if you choose.

- American Academy of Ophthalmology – **www.aao.org**
- College of Optometrists in Vision Development – **www.covd.org**
- Eye Can Learn – **www.eyecanlearn.com**
- Optometrists Network – **www.optometrists.org**
- The OT Toolbox – **www.theottoolbox.com**

Sense of Sight

"By 12 months: A child's vision reaches normal adult levels while he continues to learn about and understand what he sees" (American Academy of Pediatrics, 2012). Although a child's eyesight is functioning at adult levels, the brain must develop the ability to work as a team with the eyes and interpret and analyze what is seen. This is the difference between eyesight and vision. Eyesight is the eye's ability to see something clearly. Vison is the thought process behind what is seen.

Figure 10

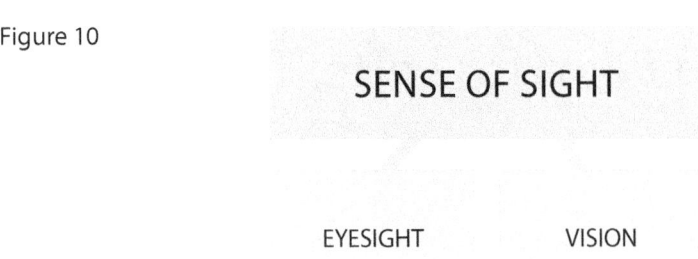

Eyesight

Eyesight is seeing clearly and in focus. It can be broken down into the following categories.

Figure 11

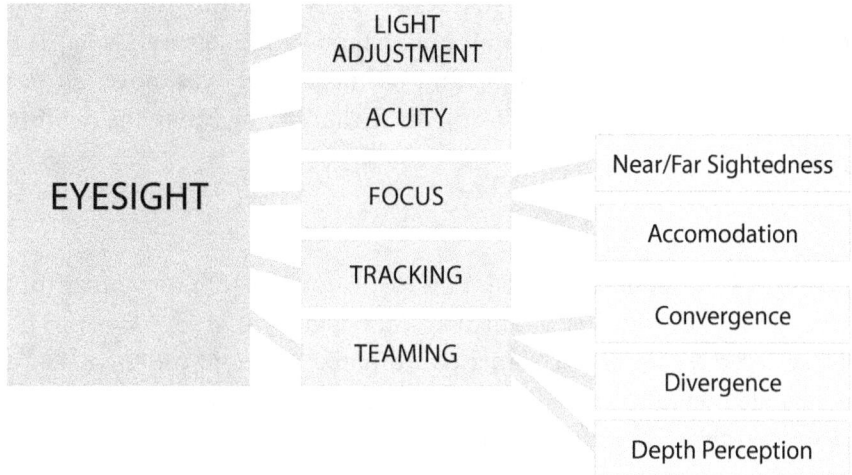

Light adjustment
Ever notice how our pupils constrict or dilate based on the level of light? This is the eyes adjusting to allow the appropriate amount of light to enter so they can see. The pupils constrict when the lights are bright and if darker, they dilate to let plenty of light in.

Acuity
Acuity refers to the sharpness and clarity of vision.

Focus
Focus is the eyes' ability to adjust to see things clearly.

Near sightedness/ Far sightedness
Near sightedness is seeing and focusing on objects up close while far sightedness is the ability to see objects clearly at a distance.

Accommodation
Accommodation involves the eyes' ability to move from one focal point to another and automatically stay in focus. This includes looking at something at a distance then shifting focus to something up close. Classrooms require this skillset as children look up at a board then quickly shift their focus down at their paper on the desk.

Tracking
"Eye tracking is foundational for reading, which, of course, requires very precise

eye control" (Connell & McCarthy, 2014). Tracking allows the eyes to follow a moving object while the head stays stationary. They smoothly shift from one fixation point to the next while the brain understands and interprets what is being seen. This skill is essential for reading and writing as our eyes move left to right then swiftly down to the next line. Problems with tracking can make reading and writing difficult.

Teaming

Also known as binocular vision, teaming is the coordinated movement of both eyes so they can work together in unison. "Binocularity (two-eyed vision) [is] the ability to sweep the eyes together in a coordinated way and use them as a team to form a single mental picture from the images that the eyes separately record, such as looking skyward with two eyes to see just one moon" (Kranowitz, 2005). When looking at a single object, each eye sends an individual picture to the brain; however, the brain does not see the two images, instead, it merges them together to see only one. This ability depends on the eyes working as a team and focusing on the object in precisely the right way. According to Angela Hanscom, issues with binocular vision are increasing. "One problem that many therapists are seeing today, as opposed to thirty years ago, is that more and more children have trouble using the muscles of their eyes in unison, say to scan a room to find an object or to read a book accurately" (Hanscom, 2016).

Convergence

"Efficient eye teaming enables the student to focus, track and concentrate when reading" (Hannaford, 2005). When looking at an object up close, our eyes move slightly inward, or converge, to assist the brain in merging the images from both eyes, into one image. This is essential for reading and writing.

Convergence insufficiency

My son Mason was diagnosed with convergence insufficiency when he turned seven years old. This means the eyes do not turn inward, or converge, when looking at an object up close. Because of this, the brain is not seeing one image, but rather double or jumpy images. My son's compensatory strategy was to cover his left eye either by putting his head on the desk, hiding his eye with his arm, or by leaning his head on his hand to cover his eye. By doing this, his brain was only seeing the image from his right eye, thus eliminating the double vision. After about a year of vision therapy and pencil pushups (where I would hold a pencil about a foot in front of his face and slowly move it to the tip of his nose and back while he followed it with his eyes), his brain and eyes started to work as a team. His left eye was retrained to move inward when seeing close objects.

- **Divergence**
Divergence is the opposite of convergence. Whereas looking at a close object, the eyes must come together, looking at a distant object requires the eyes to remain parallel to accurately focus and see. This skill comes in handy when looking at a book a teacher is reading at group time or looking at something across the room.

- **Depth perception**
Depth perception, which relies on binocular vision, is seeing in three dimensions (length, width, and depth). This helps judge distances between us and objects in the environment or between the items themselves. We use depth perception everyday as we move about the environment without running into objects or tripping over things.

Vision

"A child may pass a visual acuity eye exam and still have an undetected vision problem – mainly because 20/20 eyesight does not indicate 'perfect' functioning of the visual skills" (Lazarus, 2020). The sense of sight involves more than just seeing clearly. It requires perception for the brain to interpret and understand information coming from the eyes and visual motor integration to help the body maneuver the physical environment.

Perception

"Every eye-opening minute of the day, a child's eyes must transmit massive amounts of visual information to the brain" (Connell & McCarthy, 2014). Visual perception is the brain making sense of what is seen. It processes and gives meaning to the information the eyes bring in.

Visual attention
"Visual attention [is] using the eyes, brain, and body together long enough to stay with an activity, such as reading, following directions, or looking at an object or person" (Kranowitz, 2005). This requires discerning visual information that is important and disregarding what is irrelevant to the situation; ignoring the background distractions.

Visual discrimination

"Visual discrimination helps us refine details about what we see, where the object is in space, and where we are in relation to it" (Kranowitz, 2005). This is being able to discern characteristics amongst forms and objects including colors, sizes, shapes, and positions; an ability needed to match pictures and objects with similar characteristics. Visual discrimination also helps a person distinguish between different letters and similarly spelled words using the same letters, such as "tac" and "cat."

Visual memory

Visual memory is storing information from the eyes then retrieving the visual details either comprehensively or in a sequence. Simply put, it is remembering what has been seen or read. This affects our ability to look at a word or object then write it down without having to refer back to it. Children who struggle with this might take a long time copying something off the board, and encounter problems with reading and spelling. They may also have difficulties with

Figure 12

VISION

PERCEPTION	VISUAL MOTOR INTEGRATION
Visual Attention	Eye-Hand Coordination
Visual Discrimination	Eye-Foot Coordination
Visual Memory	Eye-Body Coordination
Spatial Relations	
Form Constancy	
Visual Closure	
Figure Ground	

remembering and reproducing a sequence of movements or motor patterns that have been shown to them. This can affect repeating motions in a music and movement class or forming letters when writing.

Spatial relations

"Spatial relations, or visual spatial awareness, refers to an organization of visual information and an awareness of position in space so the body can move and perform tasks" (Beck, 2021). This includes laterality, which is understanding there is a left and right side of one's own body (body awareness). This is also directionality, the perception of left and right for other people or objects, and comprehending that it may differ from your own. In other words, when I am looking at you, my right side is not your right side, but rather, your left. Developing a concept of positions starts with the child understanding laterality first (as it pertains to themselves), then evolves outward to relate to someone or something else; hence, the development of directionality.

Functioning in a classroom depends on spatial relations. Learning the alphabet involves understanding directionality of the letters (d/b, n/u). Children who reverse letters may struggle with spatial relationships. Think of how often tasks revolve around spatial orientation. "Put your name on the top, right corner of the page." Or "The letter J has a hook on the left side." Spatial relations are vital in the learning environment.

Form constancy

Seeing and recognizing an object, form, or symbol regardless of size, position, color, font, or texture, is form constancy. In essence, one square can be big and red, and another one can be small and blue, but they are both squares. Completing puzzles requires form constancy. We mentally manipulate the extra pieces and visualize them in different positions to see if they will fit together within the puzzle.

Form constancy is the way we recognize the same letter in different fonts; the letter A will always be the letter A regardless of its typeface. Children who struggle with form constancy may have trouble recognizing letters or reading in different fonts or colors. They may also have difficulties finding or recognizing everyday objects in different positions.

Visual closure

"Visual closure is the ability to recognize a whole object (or symbol) when only part of it is visible" (Eide & Eide, 2006). This is also recognizing that identical objects are the same even if one part of the object is missing. Children who have issues with visual closure find it hard to identify objects when only parts of the object are showing, making it hard to find items in drawers and closets. If there is a pile of clothes in the closet, and a person who struggles with visual closure is looking for a shoe, if only the heel of the shoe can be seen, that person's brain will not process and visualize the whole shoe, making it harder to find.

This is important when it comes to reading. Instead of the brain pausing and decoding each individual letter, visual closure allows us to see parts of the word and then recognize it by sight. This helps the brain become efficient in the reading process and frees up cognitive processing to comprehend the language, instead of being preoccupied with decoding. Lack of visual closure may hinder this process. "A child with visual closure difficulties will need to orientate to each letter rather than a word, making reading stilted and slow. The child may then lose the meaning of what is read" (NEPS, Report Writing Group, 2015).

Figure ground
"Visual figure ground [is] differentiating objects in the foreground and background, to distinguish one word on a page, or a face in the crowd" (Kranowitz, 2005). Reading requires figure ground as it is focusing on words being read from a page with a lot of other letters and words on it. A child with poor figure ground may get easily overwhelmed with this process.

Visual Motor Integration
When it comes the vision sense, the eyes and brain must coordinate with the entire body to function in the world. The brain receives information from the environment then tells the body how to react or respond.

Eye-hand coordination
The eyes and brain work in a coordinated effort with the hands to complete tasks such as writing and other fine motor skills. The visual input from the eyes helps guide the hands to manipulate objects such as blocks or shoelaces.

Eye-foot coordination
Eye-foot coordination happens when the brain guides the feet and helps them maneuver based on information coming in from the eyes. This skill is important for gross motor experiences and when playing sports.

Eye-body coordination
Eye-body coordination allows the entire body to function in an environment based on visual input. This informs our everyday functioning in the world such as moving around a desk or picking up a pencil on the floor.

Vision and Alphabet Knowledge

"Reading depends on the ability to visually distinguish the structural features of letters and punctuation, and how they form words, sentences, and paragraphs" (Epstein, 2014). Part of alphabet knowledge is recognizing and identifying the distinct appearance of each letter. This ability relies on the eyes seeing a unique shape and the brain processing and interpreting what letter that shape identifies. The mind must be capable of differentiating and knowing the various lines, dots, and forms that comprise each letter. This hinges on every aspect of eyesight and vision. The sense of sight is vital for learning the alphabet.

Why is this information important?
Before children can identify letters and read, their sense of sight needs to be developed. Knowing the complexities of the visual system and how each component plays a part should influence the experiences provided in the early childhood classroom. Instead of skipping steps and going straight to letter recognition, the learning environment needs to provide opportunities for vision to develop. Understanding this information helps debunk the "earlier is better" myth, and embrace building fundamental skills that will support children when they are ready to learn the letters. If stakeholders question this approach to teaching the alphabet, solid knowledge about the sense of sight provides wonderful talking points about the foundational skills that are needed first.

Experiences to Promote the Sense of Sight

Although the sense of sight is a multifaceted system, its development depends on simple authentic experiences. In other words, child-led play! This is the best opportunity for children to get continuous, hands-on, engaging experiences. Here are some ideas to implement in the classroom, to develop all the components of vision.

Child-Led Play

Why do I emphasize child-led play? Children are intuitive; their brains tell their bodies what they need, then their actions tell us. Designing an environment that is developmentally appropriate and giving children the freedom to play is the best way for children to develop their sense of sight - and everything else. While playing, children interact with their environments, utilizing their vision and eye-body coordination. They engage with three-dimensional materials that challenge all areas of visual perception as they pretend, build, and create. Child-led play naturally supports the development of vision.

Designing the Visual Environment

Create a learning environment that is visually pleasant. When there are no children in the room, it should appear neutral and almost bland. Once the children arrive with their different colors of skin, hair, clothes and bags, combined with the visual aspects of their movements, they will add the color needed to the environment. If your room is jam-packed full of wall displays, rugs, shelves, tables, and materials of bright primary colors, it will be aesthetically cluttered and overwhelming. Keep it simple. If you feel it is too bare, gradually add more, while always monitoring the children's reactions and cues.

Materials and Experiences for Learning Environments

What should be included in an environment, to support the visual system? Think hands-on, multi-sensory, and open-ended. Here are some ideas to place throughout the environment. All these materials support each category of eyesight and vision.

> *Guidelines for selecting anti-bias materials*
>
> Be intentional when selecting materials for the environment and ensure children can see themselves and also see and learn about others.
>
> "In addition to the importance of seeing themselves in their learning environment, children also learn from materials that illuminate diversity both within and beyond their own identity groups. This includes learning materials that accurately and nonstereotypcially reflect
>
> > Children and adults from the various racial and ethnic identity groups in your program and larger community

- Families from a range of economic groups performing all types of work (e.g., manual labor, office work, work in home)
- People with disabilities of various backgrounds working, playing, spending time with their families
- Diverse family structures
- People, past and present, who have enhanced the quality of life and worked for social justice in the children's own communities in the larger society" (Derman-Sparks, Edwards, & Goins, 2020).

Puzzles

Puzzles are a must as they are wonderful for eye-hand coordination, and enhance all the other visual perception skills as well. Looking for the correct puzzle piece, although it may be in a different position than the puzzle opening, enhances form constancy. Having to manipulate a piece around to make it fit is working those spatial relations skills. Puzzles provide optimal opportunities to develop the sense of sight and should be available throughout the entire environment.

Loose parts

Include loose parts of different sizes, colors, textures, and weight everywhere throughout the setting -- indoors and outdoors. Let children play with loose parts as they choose, and guide their experience. By doing this, children will engage every aspect of sight, from tracking and teaming to visual perception and motor integration skills. Pay attention to the children's interests, and make sure the materials reflect those interests. If you find the children are losing interest in the loose parts, swap them out with something else or move them to a different area of the learning environment.

Materials for tracking and eye-hand coordination

When children work with their hands, what happens with the eyes? Typically, the eyes track what the hands are doing, or they track the object the hands are manipulating. Not only does this help with eye-hand coordination, but it also develops tracking skills. (And a bonus - a lot of these materials also enhance fine motor skills.) Here are some items to place in the environment:

- Building materials
- Catapults – the eyes track the object being projected
- Craft sticks and clothespins

- Lacing items
- Marble runs
- Pegs and pegboards
- Pom-pom balls and tweezers
- Puppets – the eyes track the puppet as it moves around
- Push and pull objects - this includes cars, balls, and anything children can push and pull
- Ramps and balls – the eyes track the balls as they move

Building materials

Not only do building materials assist in eye-hand and eye-body coordination, they also support eye tracking, teaming, visual discrimination, spatial relations, form constancy, visual closure, and figure ground. The following are just a few building materials to consider for your learning environment.

- Blocks
- Lego®
- Lincoln Logs®
- Tinker Toys®
- Bristle Blocks®
- Empty boxes

Open-ended art materials

Art creation elicits an abundance of opportunities for visual stimulation and development. Keep the art area open-ended with a variety of materials to envision, design, and create. Let children express themselves as they desire with the materials provided.

Dramatic play materials

Think of all the props and tools that promote dramatic play. All these materials help develop the various aspects of eyesight and vision. Get creative. Instead of dress up clothes, use various sizes and colors of scarves along with clothes pins for children to create their own costumes. Many visual perception and visual motor integration skills will be used in the process.

Books throughout the environment

Provide a variety of quality books throughout the environment that children can freely enjoy. Give children credit and trust them with books we deem "teacher worthy" instead of the second hand, garage sale finds we tend to put out for children to handle. Find books with different illustrations so children can see variations in artwork. Provide books with actual real-life pictures. Most importantly, be available during play time to read a book one-on-one if a child requests that you do so.

"This is a teacher book"

Ever say this to a child? I have. It typically occurs after a group time experience of reading a wonderful and engaging book. Children are so enthralled; they naturally ask to look at the book during play time. A classic adult reply, "This is a teacher book." For years, this was my response. I preached to others about the importance of child-led repetition and extending the story, and I spoke fervently about following children's cues because if they ask, there is a need. Nonetheless, if a child asked to look at my treasured "teacher book," I said no.

Until one day when a child in my class asked, for about the fifth day in a row, if they could look at my book. I remember having an epiphany as I went to say no. First, this child is asking, there must be a need, and I am not meeting it. Secondly, I am conveying the message that I do not trust them. Finally, I am showing that I do not have the ability to share. Although I do not believe in forcing children to share, it is a quality to model in appropriate circumstances, and I was not doing that. So, with all my will, I handed my book over. This child was so honored to have my book that they took extra special care of it. They sat for a long time looking at it over and over again. When finished, they handed it back to me, well cared for and intact.

From then on, I didn't hesitate to let children handle and read my books. In fact, I started to place them in the literacy center after reading them at group time. I had no trouble trusting that children would handle them respectfully and return them to me in perfect condition. So, the next time a child asks, trust them, and allow them the pleasure of reading your books!

Gross motor movement materials and experiences

"Visual perception is strengthened by the vestibular activity of dancing..." (O'Connor & Daly, 2016). We need lots of gross motor movement in our programs. All day, every day! Not just during music and movement times, but the opportunity should be there through every aspect of the day and the environment. Let's encourage dancing, swinging, running, jumping, and all kinds of movement. These experiences are vital for development of visual motor integration and all areas of visual perception. Here are some experiences and materials to include in the classroom.

Crawling

"Crawling on all fours is important for visual acuity as the action helps [children] to stabilize and coordinate both eyes together, improving depth perception and binocular focus, which will be very significant for later reading and writing. The shift from looking at the floor (which is close to the eyes) with the head down and then looking out at something in the distance with the head up, whilst moving, helps develop both short and long vision and the ability to switch between the two" (O'Connor & Daly, 2016).

Crawling is so important for developing the sense of sight and the entire body. Include crawling during transitions and group times but also consider how playing on the floor during child-led play organically promotes crawling. When children build a block structure, they crawl from their creation to the shelf to grab more blocks. Children might crawl while pretending to be a baby during dramatic play. Maybe they crawl around the sandbox outside. These are just a few examples of how crawling occurs naturally during play. So, again, let children play!

Balls for bouncing, tossing, and rolling

Children benefit from all types of balls in the environment including tennis balls, kick balls, beach balls, and pretty much any ball that can be bounced, tossed, and rolled around. All support children's eye tracking, focus, spatial relations, figure ground, and visual motor integration.

Scarves and streamers

Provide different colors and lengths of scarves and streamers indoors and outdoors to encourage focus and tracking as well as spatial relations and visual motor integration. These materials can be used during group times, and can be placed around the room for children to use anytime they please.

Outside Environments and Play

Children benefit tremendously from time outdoors. "Playing outdoors can positively affect the function and growth of the eyes" (Hanscom, 2016). Recess isn't what we do when we are finished with our "inside work." Outside play is fundamental in developing all aspects of the visual system. Running and maneuvering around playground equipment develops spatial relations and visual motor integration. Chasing friends around helps with tracking and figure ground. Climbing assists with depth perception and spatial relations in addition to visual motor integration. Swinging and playing with balls enhance focus and accommodation. Natural, fun experiences outdoors develop all aspects of the sense of sight, so let's go outside!

CHAPTER THREE

Group Time Experiences for the Sense of Sight

There is a time and place for everything, including group time experiences, as long as they are developmentally appropriate, engaging, and of the children's interests. If children lose interest in a group time experience you have planned, give yourself permission to move on to something else. The following are some examples of group time experiences that promote eyesight and vision.

Read aloud

Reading aloud is a great opportunity to engage the sense of sight. Let children talk about what they see. If they recognize or notice something interesting with the illustrations, take the time to have a conversation about it. Find wordless picture books and encourage children to tell you about the pictures and what stories they think the pictures are telling.

Here are some possible books to include to promote vision.

- *A Ball for Daisy* by Chris Raschka
- *Another* by Christian Robinson
- *Have You Seen My Duckling?* by Nancy Tafuri
- *Hike* by Peter Oswald
- *Inside Outside* by Lizi Boyd
- *Field Trip to the Moon* by John Hare
- *Flashlight* by Lizi Boyd
- *Float* by Daniel Miyares
- *Flotsam* by David Wiesner
- *Flora and the Flamingo* by Molly Idle
- *Found* by Jeff Newman
- *Museum Trip* by Barbara Lehman
- *Shadow* by Suzy Lee
- *Sidewalk Flowers* by Sydney Smith
- *The Girl and the Bicycle* by Mark Pett
- *The Red Book* by Barbara Lehman
- *Tuesday* by David Wiesner
- *Wallpaper* by Thao Lam
- *Wave* by Suzy Lee
- *Where's Walrus?* by Stephen Savage

Building an anti-bias library

While making book selections, keep in mind these resources are a great way for children to see diversity and learn about others as well as see reflections of themselves. When selecting books, keep the following in mind. "Look at who is made visible in the book and who is missing. No single book covers everyone and every identity, but your collection of books should show a wide range of people by race, gender identity, family structure, economic class, culture, age, ability, and more" (Derman-Sparks, Edwards, & Goins, 2020).

The following is a great checklist for choosing and analyzing books for your setting.

"Children's books that contain accurate, nonstereotypical depictions of ...

- Physical characteristics and lives of the children, families, and staff in the program
- Different languages, especially those spoken by children, families, and staff in the program and in the community
- Diversity of gender roles, racial and cultural backgrounds, and abilities
- A range of occupations and income levels that support and supplement the diversity present in the program
- Many different family structures, so there are no token books of any particular type of family" (Derman-Sparks, Edwards, & Goins, 2020).

Finger plays

How do finger plays help with eyesight and vision? Children tend to look at our hands or their own while chanting and singing away. Finger plays are wonderful for tracking, teaming, and figure ground, along with eye-hand coordination!

Matching and sorting games

This can be done in a variety of ways utilizing different materials such as cards, manipulatives, loose parts, or almost any material. Place the items in the middle of the group or better yet, around the room, and encourage children to find the match. Be creative with this and make it as engaging and interactive as possible. A favorite of mine is scattering various pairs of socks around the room. Have children go find a sock then walk around and find the person holding the mate. When the pair is found, sort the socks into piles based on color, plain vs patterned, or long vs short.

Graphing experiences
As a group, sort objects based on visual attributes, then create a graph. This can be done in conjunction with the matching games too. Graphing also provides a wonderful opportunity to write in front of children.

Flashlight tracking
Dim the lights then shine a flashlight across the room. Have the children follow it by either pointing with their fingers or lying down on their backs and trailing it with their feet. Another option is to have them track it with just their eyes while keeping their heads still. Also consider having children close their eyes then open them to find where the flashlight is shining in the room.

Play "I Spy"
"I spy with my little eye!" Find something in the environment and describe it by its visual attributes. Encourage children to look around and guess what it is. What a fun way to enhance visual discrimination and figure ground. This experience is great for transition times.

Blow bubbles
Blow bubbles and have children catch them with their hands or kick them with their feet. This assists with focus, tracking, teaming, visual attention, spatial relations, figure ground, and visual motor integration. This is great both indoors and outside as well as a fun way to spend transition times.

Mirror motions
Move and dance around and have children mirror and mimic your movements. As they progress, do a series of moves and have the children repeat the sequence back to you. This is wonderful for visual attention, visual memory, and visual motor integration.

Experiences for Letter Recognition

We've discussed the foundations of the sense of sight, and respecting the development of all the areas of the visual system. But what about actual letter recognition, once children genuinely express an interest in the alphabet? How do we approach this in a manner that meets their developmental needs? Flash cards or "learning" apps claim to teach children letters, but teach rote memorization. Instead, follow children's cues and find opportunities to write in front of them or give visuals of letters of interest when the time is significant and right. The following are some meaningful ways to introduce letter recognition in the learning environment.

Write in Front Children

Writing in front of children while verbally saying the letters is one of the most powerful ways to cultivate alphabet knowledge and letter recognition. Describe the letters and use vocabulary to depict the visual features such as straight, curved, and squiggly. Child-led play lends itself to many opportunities to write in front of children in a manner that connects to their world. From writing about their open-ended drawings to helping spell a word they might need in a dramatic play scenario; children's play gives us the chance to write something that is important to them in that moment. What better way to see not only what the letter looks like, but how to use it purposefully?

> *Does morning message count?*
>
> It depends. Do the children in the class seem interested in the morning message? Is it relevant to the context of their worlds? Is it fun and interactive? Or is it required by your school or curriculum and done as a rote activity to check off? If it is the latter, try something else. Writing a predetermined sentence (dictated by a curriculum or theme) for children to look at and identify letters isn't a child-centered experience. Conducting morning message in this manner does not connect to children. There are more meaningful ways to model writing for children and give them opportunities to see the alphabet in action.
>
> During group times, ask children what they did last night. Write down their responses. Verbally spell some of the words while writing. Or simply ask the children what they want you to write about. If we follow children's cues and find out what is relevant to them, these experiences will be much more effective. Instead of a morning message, be available to write when children request you to do so, when it is relevant to their play. How empowering for children to see spoken words turn into print and then use them to transform a play scenario! Seizing these types of opportunities to write in front of children in a natural context resonates more with them than a scripted morning message every day.

Print Rich Environments

"Creating a print-rich environment does not mean overloading your classroom with print. Too much print can be overwhelming and can in fact create the opposite of the intended effect" (McKay & Teale, 2015). We need to make sure our rooms are print rich, not print saturated. Like everything else, this needs to be purposeful and done in ways that connect with the children in the environment. Here are some ideas for meaningful print around the room.

Label the room

Early in my career, we, as a profession, were directed to label everything in our classrooms. Everything! Soap. Trash can. Light. Chair (on every single chair). It was tedious, hard to keep up with, and overwhelming. We started to notice that the children overlooked the labels because there were too many and they didn't connect to what was important to them. All our efforts were counterproductive because labeling is only effective if it connects to children's worlds.

"There are three main kinds of environmental print you can consider including in a classroom filled with young children: labels for objects and materials and spaces, labels for children's personal possessions, and all manner of lists that help manage your day-to-day work together" (McKay & Teale, 2015). Knowing this, let's ask ourselves, what is important to the children in our setting, and label that for them. Label their names on their cubbies and coat hooks. Label with words and pictures where the materials go on the shelf when it is time to clean up. Post a daily schedule with pictures and meaningful print that children can follow along for the day. These are the labels that connect to children and should be included in a print rich environment.

Different fonts

This may go against what other specialists suggest, but I believe we should write and label in different styles, fonts, and colors. The alphabet does not exist in one form. Even in picture books, the text is written differently. Part of form constancy mentioned earlier is recognizing the same letter written in different fonts. Children will not be reading just one typeface; therefore, let's demonstrate writing as it appears in a variety of forms. Be sure to use proper capitalization and write legibly; otherwise, don't feel confined to only one way of writing. Perhaps if children see letters written in different, fun ways, it will encourage them to ask you to write something.

Alphabet charts

I am going to rock the boat here. I always had an alphabet chart in my classroom. At times, it was a poster with the entire alphabet on it. Other years, I had alphabet cards going across the top of the room as a border. This was until, as a profession, we had the epiphany to utilize wall décor for "instruction," and decided to post everything at the children's eye level. So, the following year, the border that once adorned the top of my room moved down so the children could easily see it. I did this because it had always been done and that is what I thought I was supposed to do.

The funny thing is, in over ten years of doing this, I don't ever remember children looking at those charts, using them as a reference, or even caring about them. The reason? It wasn't important to them. It wasn't of their interest. If this is so, why is decorating our rooms with the alphabet something so widely done? If it is to check off the "alphabet chart" box on the "print rich environment" checklist, this practice needs to be reconsidered. If it is just there for decoration, it is ineffective and missing the point. I believe the only time to post the alphabet on the wall, or words for that matter, is if a child asks you to do so. If a child asks to have a letter or word posted, there is a reason, and we need to do it. Otherwise, there are more meaningful ways of connecting the alphabet to the environment than putting it on the walls.

Alphabet Materials for the Learning Environment

When designing a learning environment for child-led play, materials can be offered that connect to letter recognition. Like anything, if the materials are not being used, they should be removed and replaced with something else. If the children are showing an interest, keep them in the environment for as long as needed. Placement of these resources doesn't mean children will interact with them in a "literacy based" way. They might use the material as an accessory in building or dramatic play that has nothing to do with alphabet knowledge, and that is perfectly okay. Have an open mind and respect how children decide to play with the materials. Here are some ideas for inspiration.

Plastic or foam letters
Plastic or foam letters may be placed in the sensory tub to be scooped and poured or in the manipulative area for sorting or matching. They can also be included with blocks to assist with building, dramatic play, or even the art area to glue on collages or any other creation. Start with the first letters of the children's first names and move on from there.

Letter shaped cookie cutters
Cookie cutters shaped like letters can be used with paint, playdough, and in sensory tubs with sand or mud. Consider placing them in the dramatic play area

for pretending to cook or whatever else the children come up with. What about letter shaped cookie cutters outside for the sandbox? The ideas are endless.

Letter blocks

Place these in the block center for added decoration to building projects, or in the manipulative area for sorting and matching. Letter blocks are versatile and can be used anywhere in the setting.

Alphabet cutouts

Cut letters out of construction or any other type of paper. Add scissors and glue and let children cut the letters apart and glue the pieces to any art creation they choose to make. Laminate the letters and cut holes around the edge for lacing. Place them with tape in the block area so children can adhere letters to any block structure for additional decoration.

Alphabet puzzles

Place alphabet puzzles throughout the environment for children to experience the formations and shapes of the letters. Ensure the puzzle has a space for each letter; if each individual letter is its own puzzle piece, it allows children to feel the shape of just that letter. If the puzzle is just a picture of the alphabet cut into jigsaw pieces, the child will not have the opportunity to experience the individual letter.

Letter sorts and matches

Letter sorts and matches can be done a variety of ways. For this to be effective, children must have an interest in not only the alphabet, but the specific letters used in the experience. In other words, if you create a letter sort or match experience, you don't have to use the entire alphabet. What letters do the children show an interest in? Use those letters then go from there. Match the exact letters or the upper to lower case. What about matching the letters in different fonts? Just ensure that whatever is created connects to the children.

> *Call it what it is*
>
> Resist the urge to require participation in the following experiences and call it play. Call that what it is, a "hands-on, teacher-directed" activity. If the adult designs it and mandates the child to complete it, that is not play.

My intent in sharing these is not to give ideas for teacher-directed time, but to suggest materials to place in the environment for children to play with if they choose to do so. If children play with the materials differently than you expected, that is fine. These are options and choices, not requirements. If you find children are not engaging with the materials, take the items out of the environment because they are not serving a purpose.

Towel tube and stickers
Write letters on a paper towel tube and the corresponding letters on circle stickers. Place the letter stickers onto the matching letters on the paper towel tube.

Cars and parking garage
Write letters on Matchbox® cars. Create a parking lot with corresponding letters on a piece of poster board. Park the car on the matching letter.

Balls and craft rolls
Write letters on plastic balls and corresponding letters on cardboard craft rolls. Balance the matching ball on top of the correct tube.

Paper plate and clothespins
Write letters around the edge of a paper plate. Write corresponding letters on clothespins. Place the clothespins around the plate on the correct letter.

Alphabet books

It might not surprise you that I don't always have a favorable view on alphabet books. These are books where the entire story revolves around the alphabet, or the illustrations represent each letter of the alphabet. Many curriculum companies have published books that coordinate with the alphabet or a specific letter. Some of these books are enjoyable and make for a fun read aloud. Other times, they are boring and serve the purpose of checking off the "alphabet rich literature in the classroom" box. As with anything, read the children's cues. If you put an alphabet book in the environment or read it at group time and they don't seem interested, move on to something else. Making children endure a book they don't find interesting will not teach them the alphabet.

On the other hand, when it comes to alphabet books children do love, be realistic in the purpose they serve. Instead of tools to "teach" the letters, I view them as opportunities to experience the alphabet in a meaningful context. A great example is *Chicka Chicka Boom Boom* by Bill Martin, Jr. and John Archambault.

Children enjoy this book and I do too. (See Chapter 4 on phonological awareness because I think it is one of the best pieces of literature addressing phonemes and sounds.) If you have read this book, you know how children respond. They wait and anticipate the part of the story that has "their letter," then they scream in excitement, "That's me! That's my letter!" As they start to learn their family and friends' letters, they wait to point those out too. This book provides a wonderful chance to recognize letters important to children in an enjoyable manner, making it fun and effective.

Just say no to flashcards

Flashcards can be a form of surface teaching. Think of the made-up letters at the beginning of the book. You were probably able to memorize them, but did you really learn them? Not really, because you had no connection to them, and they didn't serve a purpose in your life. Drilling children with alphabet flashcards does not result in true knowledge. It is time to move beyond this ineffective practice.

Learning to identify and name letters begins with the visual system. Focus on that first. Then, find meaningful ways for children to experience letters significant to their lives in a developmentally appropriate manner. This is how children truly learn the alphabet.

Why do these experiences work?

Before children can differentiate the individual letters of the alphabet, they need to develop their sense of sight. To develop all components of this, children need to interact in a play environment where they can move about and manipulate real, three-dimensional objects. Then, as the ability to recognize letters begins to emerge, adults can provide opportunities for children to experience the alphabet in a meaningful context. This process resonates more with children when it is done in a natural manner that connects to their play and is driven by their interests and curiosities.

WHOLE CHILD ALPHABET

CHAPTER FOUR

Letter Sounds Begin with Phonemic Awareness

What is the most amusing noise you can make? Do you recall being little and creating all kinds of sounds? As a child, I remember pretending with my friends to be opera singers and trying to get our voices as high and loud as possible. I also remember us imitating the sounds of cars and motorcycles because in our minds it made the make-believe play realistic. And nothing made us happier than nailing a difficult tongue twister. This may seem silly, but these experiences were helping our brains develop phonological awareness, a critical component of the literacy process, and for recognizing and identifying the unique sounds for each letter of the alphabet.

Letter Sounds Start Somewhere

The cornerstone of reading and spelling is phonological awareness, which is the ability to hear, decipher, and manipulate the sounds of language. This is also separating the meaning of language from the sounds of the words. "Phonological awareness is sensitivity to the sound structure of language. It demands the ability to turn one's attention to sounds in spoken language while temporarily shifting away from its meaning" (Yopp & Yopp, 2009). Although we can facilitate opportunities that promote phonological awareness, it really is a skill that is developed through playing and experiencing true, authentic sounds and voices.

Phonological Awareness and Its Components

Have you ever heard a language you are not familiar with, and it sounds like a cluster of sounds that you can't quite make out? But as you learn the language, your brain becomes attuned to the phonemes and rhythms of the language, making it easier to decipher the words and decode the meanings. Phonological awareness for young children works in much the same way. Children hear the language as a whole and as their brains start to develop phonological awareness, they start to distinguish words and individual sounds within what is being said. This helps them to not only understand, but also to isolate and produce the sounds of language.

Think of phonological awareness as a larger-to-smaller process. It starts with being aware of sounds and works its way into recognizing the rhythms and rhymes of language. Children develop the ability to hear words in sentences then eventually break those words into syllables. The next step is dividing the syllables into onset and rime units. With time and experience, the brain refines this process, which culminates in being able to detect the smallest unit of sound, the phoneme. When children can manipulate the phonemes by blending them together and taking them apart, they are ready for reading and writing.

Figure 13 shows the development of phonological awareness and how it progresses from hearing larger units of language to deciphering the smallest sounds. It's worth mentioning that although there are stages in how this develops, it's okay for children to have experiences connected to any aspect of phonological awareness. "Although instruction should generally progress from larger to smaller units of sound, phonological awareness development is not lockstep and children need not master one level before being exposed to other levels of phonological awareness" (Yopp & Yopp, 2009). For instance, it's okay to sing to an infant emphasizing rhymes and alliteration although they are in the beginning stages of sound awareness and production. A four-year-old may not have the ability to segment sounds in a word, but we still can demonstrate sounding out a word when spelling and writing it for them.

Some skills mentioned might pertain to children older than the age group in your setting. This is not to encourage skipping steps, but to recognize what phonological awareness entails and how it supports future reading and writing.

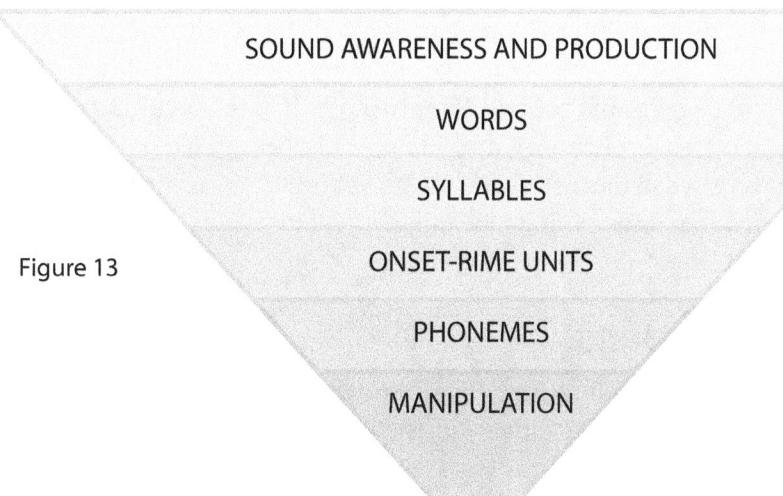

Figure 13

Sound Awareness and Production

Sound awareness and production, essentially listening and speaking, is the simplest form of phonological awareness. This begins in infancy when babies listen to us talk, then babble and coo back. It's also when toddlers and preschoolers create noises, sounds, and nonsense words during play time. During this stage, children begin to tune in to the rhythms and intonations of language, including recognizing tones, volumes, and pitches of voices.

Words

The next level of phonological awareness is the understanding that spoken language is comprised of various words. "In spoken interaction, the natural focus of very young children's attention is on comprehension, making meaning from the combination of words in a speech stream. In the acquisition of phonological awareness, children's attention therefore needs to shift from a single focus on meaning to a broader focus that also attends to individual words" (Neaum, 2017). When this emerges, children typically start to ask about words, engage in word play, and begin to recognize words that rhyme.

Syllable Awareness

"The ability to discern syllables occurs early in the developmental progression of phonological awareness" (Yopp & Yopp, 2009). Syllables are the largest sound units in words; syllable awareness is understanding that words can be divided into syllables. The emergence of this ability is the beginning step in shifting from the meaning of language, to the sounds. Simply put, when the focus moves from the word as a whole to broken down syllables, it is being analyzed based on sounds, not what the word means. Therefore, the child begins to think about the sounds of the word, separate from its meaning.

Onset and Rime Units

The next stage is understanding that syllables can be divided into two parts, onset and rime units. The onset unit is all the sounds (consonants) before the vowel in the syllable. Words that start with vowels don't have onsets. Rime units consist of the vowel and any of the sounds that follow the onset. Some words may only have a vowel as the rime unit if no consonants follow. Here are some examples of onset-rime units.

Figure 14

Word	Onset	Rime
cow	/c/	/ow/
glad	/gl/	/ad/
to	/t/	/o/
oh	(no onset)	/o/
booklet	/b/ (first syllable) /l/ (second syllable)	/ook/ (first syllable) /et/ (second syllable)

Phonemic Awareness

"Phonemic awareness is one aspect (and the most difficult) of phonological awareness. It is the ability to attend to and manipulate phonemes, the smallest sounds in speech" (Yopp & Yopp, 2009).

Phonemes are the smallest units of sound that exist. Our ability when it comes to hearing these sounds and translating them into language is astonishing. When you step back and think about it, words are just various combinations of phonemes that our brains learn to decode and connect with their meaning. When we hear the phoneme combination of /d/ /o/ /g/, our brains hear "dog," and we decipher the message being conveyed.

Phonemes of different languages

Phonemes universally exist, but they differ from language to language. "The number of sounds in speech varies greatly among languages, from as few as about 10 phonemes in Múra-Pirahã (spoken in a region of Brazil) to more than 140 phonemes in !Xu (spoken in a region of Africa). English speakers use about 44 sounds. Spanish speakers use about 24" (Yopp & Yopp, 2009). Amazingly, the human brain at birth has the ability to hear and produce any phoneme that exists in the world. "At birth, the baby brain has an unusual gift: it can tell the difference between all 800 sounds. This means that at this stage, infants can learn any language that they're exposed to. Gradually babies figure out which sounds they are hearing the most. Between 6 and 12 months, infants who grow up in monolingual households become more specialized in the subset of sounds in their native language. In other words, they become 'native language specialists.' And, by their first birthdays, monolingual infants begin to lose their ability to hear the differences between foreign language sounds" (Ramirez, 2016).

Phonemic awareness and the brain

Remember discussing brain development earlier? Experiences wire the brain; repetition strengthens the wiring. This applies to phonemic awareness as well. For children to develop the ability to hear and produce phonemes, they must experience them! This means they need to hear real, in person, human voices over and over. Not digital, artificial voices, but actual, genuine voices. Through continual exposure to people talking, children's brains strengthen the pathways for language development and phonemic awareness. That may seem basic for such a complex process, but a fascinating thing about the brain is how simple experiences are fundamental to its development. Let's look at how this works.

The brain is wired for survival and likes to keep its processes lean; it needs to build and strengthen what is essential for life and discard the "excess matter." "Connections that don't become strong through repetition get 'pruned away' – it's as if the brain prioritizes what is most useful (i.e., being used the most) and doesn't hang on to the rest" (O'Connor & Daly, 2016). If a child is experiencing language repeatedly, the brain says, "Hey, I keep hearing these [English] sounds over and over. These are important to survive in my environment. I need to strengthen the ability to hear and produce these sounds. But - I'm not hearing any [French] sounds so I don't need those to survive. Because of that, I am going to deplete the ability to hear the [French] sounds and work on building and strengthening the ability to hear [English] sounds." This is why it is imperative for children to hear an abundance of language from adults and peers, so their brains can create and reinforce the connections to isolate and produce phonemes.

It is very important to note that phonemic awareness is an elaborate process that cannot develop without exposure to authentic language experiences. Overly structured and pre-planned activities do not provide this for children; the best thing to do is encourage children to talk and to play!

Resisting digital technology for the sake of phonemic awareness

When we understand how the brain develops the ability to hear and produce phonemes, it reinforces the importance of being face-to-face with young children and having lots of conversations with them. If children are not hearing the sounds of language, their brains will not develop the ability to hear, understand, and produce those sounds. No literacy curriculum with scripts or prescribed activities can replace authentic conversations. No app can replace that either.

Which leads us to digital technology. When children are "plugged in" to a device, they lose the opportunity to hear and listen to authentic sounds in their environments. When I took my own children to the grocery store before handheld devices existed, they were hearing real sounds while making eye contact with others. This resulted in people stopping and talking to them which was wonderful, because not only were my children hearing more language and vocabulary, but they were also hearing voices that differed from mine in tone, cadence, and pitch. They also heard a variety of sounds including doors opening and closing, beeps of the cash registers, and squeaky wheels on the shopping carts. All these experiences were critical and helped their brains develop phonological awareness, including the ability to hear phonemes. If Ithey had been using a device with headphones, these experiences would not have happened, and these opportunities would have been lost.

Will digital technology be a part of children's lives from now on? Absolutely. Is it the real world for children? Yes. Should it replace human interaction and experiences? No! And that is what is happening. We as adults get distracted by digital devices, or we intentionally distract children with them, and this prevents actual conversations from happening. We know that children do not need digital devices to grow and develop, but they do need human interaction and relationships, to thrive. So, for the sake of language development, and overall child development, let's limit the use of screens and encourage children to be engaged with the real world.

Manipulation of Sound Units

Once children can hear and produce phonemes, they can start to manipulate them. Words can be created by blending the sounds and putting them together.

Segmentation consists of separating and breaking words down into individual sounds. Manipulating sound units also consists of deleting or substituting sounds in words. (For example, deleting a sound in the word would be saying "dog" without the /d/ sound – "og." Substituting sounds would be saying the word "dog" but with an /f/ sound instead of a /d/ – "fog.") If a child achieves this level of phonological awareness, imagine how prepared they will be for reading and writing.

Comprehensive View of Phonological Awareness

Before looking at phonemic awareness and alphabet knowledge, let's apply all the levels of phonological awareness to the word "chipmunk."

Figure 15

Word	chipmunk						
Syllables	chip			munk			
Onset and Rime Units	ch	ip		m	unk		
Phonemes	ch	i	p	m	u	n	k

Phonemic Awareness and Alphabet Knowledge

Why is phonemic awareness important when it comes to alphabet knowledge? "This ability, which we call phonemic awareness, is necessary in order to pair a sound to its symbol" (Christakis, 2016). Letters represent sounds, which helps translate speech into written form; however, before children can assign sounds to letters, they must be able to isolate and produce those sounds. "To learn letter-sound correspondence, which is essential to learning to read, children must become aware of phonemes" (Neaum, 2017).

Phonemes and Letters

When looking at phonemes and the alphabet, it is important to recognize that although many of our letters represent one phoneme, some of them represent two. Sometimes, the rules of phonics kick in when combining two or three letters resulting in one phoneme. Here is a simple breakdown of letters and phonemes.

Figure 16

Word	Letters	Phonemes	Explanation
Band	B-A-N-D	/b/ /a/ /n/ /d/	4 letters, 4 phonemes Each letter represents 1 phoneme
Stick	S-T-I-C-K	/s/ /t/ /i/ /k/	5 letters, 4 phonemes Letters CK together represent the phoneme /k/
Fox	F-O-X	/f/ /o/ /k/ /s/	3 letters, 4 phonemes Letter X represents 2 phonemes /k/ /s/
Shush	S-H-U-S-H	/sh/ /u/ /sh/	5 letters, 3 phonemes Letters SH together represent the phoneme /sh/

Phonemic awareness and literacy

Without phonemic awareness, children will have difficulty with not only alphabet knowledge but reading and writing in general. "We must be able to notice and have a firm grasp of the sounds of our speech if we are to understand how to use a written system that records sounds. Individuals who are unaware that speech is made up of small sounds – those who don't notice and cannot mentally grab hold of and manipulate them – have difficulty learning to read a written system based on sounds. A child's ability to reflect on language itself, specifically the sounds of language and especially the phonemes, supports the child's understanding of the logic of the written code. That we use symbols to represent small sounds **makes sense** because the English language consists of small sounds" (Yopp & Yopp, 2009). It is important in our learning environments that we provide the opportunity for children to experience and play with sounds. This is the only way phonemic awareness develops and it is vital for literacy development.

Why is this information important?

Many buy into the "earlier is better" myth when it comes to literacy. This is an area where the lines between emerging skills and developmental delays have become blurred and muddled. To explain what is developmentally appropriate, it is important to understand the fundamentals of reading and how they develop. This includes phonological awareness.

Knowing the sounds of the alphabet hinges on children's ability to isolate and produce phonemes, the most complex component of phonological awareness. Unless children hear and experience authentic sounds, this will not develop. Being able to articulate this developmental process, and why it is critical for literacy, assists us in conversations with stakeholders. Instead of giving in to a program that pushes academics on children before they are ready, this information gives us the evidence needed to advocate for play and help others understand why it is essential to children learning to read.

Experiences to Develop Phonological Awareness

Children need a phonologically rich environment. What does this look like in the classroom? Here are some experiences that support the development of phonological awareness.

Child-Led Play

The best opportunity for hearing a variety of sounds is during child-led play! Limiting play decreases children's exposure to authentic sounds in their environments, which adversely affects phonological awareness. Child-guided play provides an enormous number of noises including friends' voices, and the natural sounds created by toys and materials. If we fill our days with teacher-directed activities, this sound is minimized. Instead, allow for lots of play. If stakeholders ask why the children are playing so much, seize the opportunity to explain how play develops phonological awareness and why that is essential for alphabet knowledge and literacy.

Designing Environments for Phonological Awareness

Conversations aplenty
Conversations galore, plentiful, abounding. Whatever word is needed to describe an overabundance of children talking to us and each other, use it. Language and phonological awareness do not develop in quiet spaces. "In fact, a key component

of learning to read involves learning, first, to listen. In order to become proficient communicators, preschoolers need lots of practice hearing the small differences in sounds, which, in turn, involves conversing with others" (Christakis, 2016). Children need to talk. And not scripted conversations some curriculums provide, but true, authentic, child-inspired conversations. So, design an environment and a space that inspires children to talk, and values what they have to say.

Explore range of voice

At the beginning of the chapter, I mentioned my childhood friends and I creating various noises while playing; this is a great example of exploring different ranges of our voices! The following are some ideas for the environment that encourage children to make a variety of sounds during play.

No batteries!

A wonderful way to encourage children to play around with their voices is to provide materials with no batteries. What motivates a child to make noises if the toy does it for them? If a child is playing with a pretend train that creates a "choo-choo" sound at the push of a button, the child does not need to make that sound. But, if the train does not make the noise, the child will feel more compelled to vocalize the "choo-choo," "chug-chug," and possibly "whoo-whoo" sounds, a great way to play with their voice. As the saying goes, "the more passive the toy, the more active the child." Let's seek materials that require more of the child and support phonological awareness.

Dramatic play props

When children play with dramatic play props or act out a scenario, they alter their voices. If they're pretending that a baby doll is sleeping, they may speak quietly. If they're playing with a puppet they perceive as a grownup, they might make their voices deeper and louder. Children will change their volume, tone, and pitch for the benefit of pretend play. Generating these sounds, and hearing others do so as well, is great for phonological awareness. Place costumes, puppets, dolls, and small world props around the environment to elicit the exploration of voices.

Please refer to Chapter 3 for guidelines on selecting anti-bias materials.

Real books

If a book makes noises with the push of a button, why should the child? Pretending to be the characters or narrating illustrations is another natural opportunity to play around with sounds and voices. Have real, authentic books throughout the setting for children to look at and read. This is not limited to just the literacy center. Place books in all learning areas of the environment.

- **Materials to Alter Voice**
Provide materials in the classroom that assist in altering the voice. Here are some ideas:

  - Phoneme/ auditory feedback phones (these can be made from PVC pipe)
  - Megaphones
  - Wrapping paper tubes
  - Paper towel tubes
  - Craft rolls
  - Empty oatmeal containers
  - Empty coffee cans
  - Plastic cups
  - Hold nose while talking
  - Cup hands around mouth to make louder
  - Cup hands on and around ears to change how it sounds to self
  - Place the tip of fingers of one hand to the bottom of the palm on the other. Cup bottom hand over the mouth and cup other hand over the ear. When speaking, the hands catch the sound and allows it to travel directly to the ear.

- **Outdoors**
Being outdoors is the perfect chance to explore different volumes and pitches; it is also the ideal setting for children to get loud. Add some of the above-mentioned materials to the outdoor learning environment, too.

Instruments and noisemakers

Place instruments and noisemakers throughout the classroom for children to experience. Not digital versions, but real, genuine instruments. If it's too much or too loud for your room, have a basket that you take outside.

Sounds in the environment

Ever been in the middle of a read aloud book and the garbage truck pulls up outside your classroom window and the children lose interest in the story and run to look out the window? Instead of being flustered, embrace this moment. Call attention to the sounds heard throughout the environment such as vacuum cleaners, lawnmowers, swings squeaking, whatever it may be, and talk about what you hear.

Intentional background music

Music is a wonderful, necessary addition to the classroom. But like everything else, we need to be intentional when music is in the background while children are playing. Music sets the tone of environment. If there is high energy music on, it's going to energize the children. If there is relaxing music, it's going to calm the room down. Therefore, when children are playing, have classical music or soft jazz playing in the background, or no music at all.

> *Save sing-along songs for group times*
>
> The goal is to design an environment that promotes lots of language and discussions during play. If music with vocals and catchy lyrics is playing in the background, it can distract and sidetrack conversations. Instead, save sing-along songs for transitions and movement times.

Group Time

"When teachers introduce children to multiple experiences with oral language and systematically engage them in activities such as alliteration and rhyming, they help children develop the skills to become readers and writers" (Epstein, 2014). Group times can be beneficial for phonological awareness as long as they don't engulf the day or interfere with child-led play. Group times should be of the children's interests and connect to their ecosystems, rather than following a predetermined curriculum. Observe children, plan group times accordingly, then follow their cues when you are in the moment. Whether with a small group or one child, opportunities may spontaneously arise that lead to phonological awareness experiences.

CHAPTER FOUR

Read books with a variety of sounds

Read books embellished with a variety of sounds. Consider books with onomatopoeias, rhythm and rhymes, alliterations, and predictable text. Story time doesn't have to be quiet. Make it active and let the children immerse themselves in the books. Encourage children to pretend to be the characters and act out the stories. Prompt the children to re-create the sounds they hear. Pause while reading and see if they can predict the rhyme or word that comes next. Most importantly, follow the children's cues! My philosophy is, if children request to repeat something, there is a reason, and there is a need, so we should do it. Therefore, read, reread, and read a book again if the children request to do so!

Looking for some books that promote phonological awareness? Here are some books to read at group time and place throughout the entire learning environment. They are broken down into three groups (rhyme and rhythm, variety of sounds and alliterations, and predictable text), but many fit into multiple categories. Find what the children connect with and go from there.

Please refer to Chapter 3 for suggestions on building an anti-bias library.

Rhyme and rhythm

- *All the World* by Liz Garton Scanlon
- *Barnyard Dance!* by Sandra Boynton
- *Bee-bim Bop!* by Linda Sue Park
- *F is for Fart: A rhyming ABC children's book about farting animals* by J. Heitsch
- *Giraffes Can't Dance* by Giles Andreae
- *Green is a Chile Pepper* by Roseanne Greenfield Thong
- *Happy in Our Skin* by Fran Manushkin
- *Honey, I Love* by Eloise Greenfield
- *I Like Myself!* by Karen Beaumont
- *La Princesa and the Pea* by Susan Middleton Elya
- *Little You* by Richard Van Camp
- *Mary Had a Little Jam: And Other Silly Rhymes* by Bruce Lansky

- *One Is a Piñata* by Roseanne Greenfield Thong
- *Pete the Cat and the Cool Cat Boogie* by Kimberley and James Dean
- *Quack and Count* by Keith Baker
- *Round is a Tortilla* by Roseanne Greenfield Thong
- *Sweetest Kulu* by Celina Kalluk
- *Summer Days and Nights* by Wong Herbert Yee
- *The Way I Feel* by Janan Cain
- *Way Out in the Desert* by T. J. Marsh

<u>Variety of sounds and alliterations</u>

- *Bob, Not Bob!* by Liz Garton Scanlon and Audrey Vernick
- *Chrysanthemum* by Kevin Henkes
- *Click Clack Moo, Cows That Type* by Doreen Cronin
- *Don't Blink!* by Amy Krouse Rosenthal
- *Fry Bread: A Native American Family Story* by Kevin Noble Maillard and Juana Martinez-Neal
- *Hush! A Thai Lullaby* by Minfong Ho
- *I Got the School Spirit* by Connie Schofield-Morrison
- *Moo, Baa, La La La!* by Sandra Boynton
- *Mmm, Cookies!* by Robert Munsch
- *Run Wild* by David Covell
- *Splat!* by Jon Burgerman
- *Summer Supper* by Rubin Pfeffer
- *Tap Tap Boom Boom* by Elizabeth Bluemle
- *The Book with No Pictures* by B.J. Novak
- *The Cow Who Clucked* by Denise Fleming
- *The Hula-Hoopin' Queen* by Thelma Lynne Godin
- *The Wheels on the Tuk Tuk* by Kabir Sehgal

- *Too Much Glue* by Jason Lefebvre
- *Yo! Yes?* by Chris Raschka
- *Your Name Is a Song* by Jamilah Thompkins-Bigelow

Predictable text

- *Brown Bear, Brown Bear, What Do You See?* by Bill Martin, Jr.
- *Chicka Chicka Boom Boom* by Bill Martin, Jr. and John Archambault
- *Cock-a-Doodle Doo! Barnyard Hullabaloo* by Giles Andreae
- *Goodnight Moon* by Margaret Wise Brown
- *I Got the Rhythm* by Connie Schofield-Morrison
- *I Know a Shy Fellow Who Swallowed a Cello* by Barbara S. Garriel
- *I Say a Little Prayer for You* by Hal David and Burt Bacharach
- *If You Give a Mouse a Cookie* by Laura Numeroff
- *In the Small, Small Pond* by Denise Fleming
- *Not a Box* by Antoinette Portis
- *One Love* by Cedella Marley
- *Rap a Tap Tap: Here's Bojangles - Think of That!* by Leo and Diane Dillon
- *Stand Tall, Molly Lou Melon* by Patty Lovell
- *Subway* by Anastasia Suen
- *The Little Old Lady Who Was Not Afraid of Anything* by Linda D. Williams
- *The Napping House* by Audrey Wood
- *Big Machines! Big Buildings!* by Kevin Lewis
- *The Very Hungry Caterpillar* by Eric Carle
- *We're Going on a Bear Hunt* by Helen Oxenbury and Michael Rosen
- *Whoever You Are* by Mem Fox

Read, reread, and read again

One of my favorite books to read at group time was *Mmm, Cookies!* by Robert Munsch. It was fun, interactive, and full of interesting sounds. While reading, we would pretend to make cookies alongside the main characters. We slapped our hands together and said, "whap, whap, whap." We pretended to sprinkle sugar while saying, "chik, chik, chik." We then clasped our hands together like squeezing a tube of icing and said, "glick, glick, glick." I encouraged the children to be expressive and loud, so it was not surprising they always requested this book. (A great example of child-led repetition in a meaningful context.) I read and reread *Mmm, Cookies!* many times, knowing that experiences wire the brain and repetition strengthens the wiring. This was an effective and enjoyable way to support phonological awareness.

Listen to books without looking at the pictures

My grandparents grew up before the invention of televisions. They listened to stories and programs on the radio. Without pictorial representation, they had to imagine what everything looked like in their minds. Today, the world is inundated with visual stimulation, so there rarely is an opportunity to just listen. Try reading a book without showing the pictures. I did this at the beginning of nap time as the children were settling in on their nap mats. I encouraged them to envision the stories in their heads. Not only did this develop visual imagery, but it also provided opportunities to rely solely on the auditory sense. When nap was over, I read the book again and showed them the pictures. The conversations about how the children imagined the story versus the illustrator's interpretation were fascinating.

Songs and finger plays

Sing a variety of songs and finger plays in an engaging and energetic way. Get up, move around, and be as active as possible.

Nursery rhymes

Although the prose and rhythm of nursery rhymes are ideal for developing phonological awareness, many are outdated or offensive. Research and apply the same guidelines for selecting anti-bias books to picking nursery rhymes, before introducing them to the children.

Emphasize rhyme through movement

During group times or transitions, emphasize rhyming sounds in songs with various movements. A wonderful example is "Twinkle, Twinkle, Little Star." Stand while singing or chanting, and jump into a star formation (or star jump) every time the word "star," or a word that rhymes with "star," is heard.

>Twinkle, twinkle, little star, (**star jump**)
>How I wonder what you are. (**star jump**)
>Up above the world so high,
>Like a diamond in the sky.
>
>Twinkle, twinkle, little star. (**star jump**)
>How I wonder what you are. (**star jump**)

Expect everyone to get into the rhythm of the song and star jump on the words "high" and "sky." This opens the opportunity to discuss whether "high" and "sky" rhyme with "star," and everyone listens more closely to the sounds, after this happens.

Music

- **Clap to songs**
  Breaking songs down into beats and rhythms correlates to breaking language down into phonological units. Clap, march, and dance to songs, emphasizing the beats and rhythms.

- **Freeze dance**
  Play music and dance. When the music stops, everyone freezes. When the music continues, so does the dancing. Not only does this hone the listening skills, but it also works on impulse control.

- **Sing a cappella**
  Although we have access to wonderful, prerecorded music, it is harder to hear yourself and others sing if you have to battle the blaring music in the background. Since being able to hear actual human voices is key to phonemic awareness, save the prerecorded music for movement experiences.

Creating sounds

Ever wonder how bodies can physically create language? It is incredible that pulling air from the lungs, then manipulating the vocal cords, teeth, tongue, and lips, generates sounds. Use your hands to feel how the mouth and vocal cords do this. It's not only fascinating, but it helps children be aware of how they produce and manipulate sounds with their bodies. How is this done?

Place one hand in front of the mouth and the other hand on the front of the neck.

Make the /p/ sound over and over. What do you feel? On the hand in front of your mouth, you should feel air hitting your hand. The hand on your neck might feel slight movement, but nothing significant. Air is being pulled from the lungs and the lips come together to stop the air. This is how we make the /p/ sound.

Place your hands back in front of your mouth and neck and repeat the /p/ sound over and over. Leaving your hands in place, change the /p/ sound to the /b/ sound. What did you notice? The mouth doesn't change and the air on the hand in front of the mouth feels the same; however, the hand on the neck should feel vibration. This is because we make the /p/ and /b/ sounds the same way except the /p/ is voiceless and the /b/ is voiced. Therefore, the vocal cords are turned on for the /b/ sound which accounts for the vibration felt on the neck.

Try this again with a variety of other voiced and voiceless sounds. Here are a few things to draw attention to:

- /t/ and /d/ - Sounds created by stopping the air with the tongue behind the teeth and turning the voice on and off.
- /k/ and /g/ - Sounds made by stopping air with the tongue at the back of the mouth and turning the voice on and off.
- /f/ and /v/ - Sounds shaped by streaming air through the upper teeth and bottom lip and turning the voice on and off.
- /s/ and /z/ - Sounds created by streaming air with tongue behind the upper teeth (but not touching the teeth) and turning the voice on and off.
- /m/ and /n/ - These are nasal sounds meaning the air comes out of the nose, not the mouth, as the sound is made. For /m/, the lips block the air and for /n/, the tongue blocks it. When

placing hands on the mouth and neck, vibration on the neck can be felt, but nothing on the hand in front of the mouth because the air is coming from the nose. Try doing this then hold your nose. What happens? The sound stops because the nose is blocked, and the air has nowhere to go!

- All vowel sounds are made with the vocal cords, so they are considered voiced.

Other ways to play with sounds:

- Hold the nose for all sounds.
- Place hands over ears to amplify the voiced sounds. Compare to voiceless sounds.
- Put paper or tissue in front of the mouth to see it move for voiceless sounds. Compare to voiced sounds.
- Break down sounds of children's names to see how it feels to create them. This will provide the opportunity to explore a variety of phonemes that exist by combining letters. Examples: CH = /ch/, SH = /sh/, TH = /th/
- Provide mirrors throughout the environment so children can visually see what their mouths look like while talking.

Some great discussion points when doing this:

- How does the air feel flowing out of the mouth? Does it stop or feel continuous?
- What part of the mouth moves to make the sounds?
- What do we notice about the sounds when the vibration is felt on the neck? (When the vibration is felt, that means the vocal cords are making the sounds.)
- What about changing the pitch of the voice and making it go higher or lower? What makes that happen? (The vocal cords move faster to make high sounds and move slower for low sounds.)
- How does the volume change for the sounds? (More air from the lungs creates louder sounds while less air results in quieter sounds.)

Creating syllables

Place hand under chin while talking to feel how the mouth moves when making different syllables. Also clap out syllables to emphasize them in words.

Nonsense rhymes

Give a word and have the children generate a rhyming word. They won't always be actual words, and many times they will be very silly, but that is okay as long as it rhymes.

Clapping game

This can be done a variety of ways during group times as well as transitions. The premise is to clap at different volumes. When getting louder, the children stand. As the clapping gets softer, children sit. Another idea is to adjust the rate of clapping. The children stand when the clapping is faster and sit as the clapping gets slower. This can also be done with instruments or other materials from the environment.

Guess that sound

Have children close their eyes if they are comfortable doing so. Play or create a sound (an instrument, a noise maker, or any other object) and let them guess what it is. The goal is for the children to not rely on their visual sense, but depend solely on their listening skills. This is where digital technology can be useful as it provides sounds of objects that might not be in the classroom such as trains, oceans, or animals. Keep in mind the children's backgrounds. What sounds are they familiar with? What will make sense to them? If new sounds are played, this creates the opportunity to discuss sound association (relating a new sound to a familiar one). Is the unfamiliar sound like a familiar one? What does it sound like, that we are familiar with? Are the objects that make those sounds similar? This lends itself to some interesting conversations with children providing fun and creative descriptions.

> *The case against early phonics curriculum and instruction*
>
> In an effort to promote reading skills, many programs introduce phonics-based curriculums at an early age that tend to skip critical steps and may not support phonological awareness. "Phonics, which is not the same as phonological or phonemic awareness, is a system of teaching how letters

and combinations of letters correspond to sounds of spoken language and is typically introduced in kindergarten or first grade" (NAEYC, 2009). Many of these curriculums are actually designed for elementary-aged children and do not meet the developmental needs of children still in preschool.

Phonics-based programs are one of many examples of pushing elementary academics down on preschoolers and toddlers for the sake of school readiness. Many of these curriculums claim to teach children their letters and sounds to give them a head start on reading. Unfortunately, many of these activities take time away from the child-led play needed for phonological awareness. Instead of getting them ahead, these programs run the risk of children falling behind because they do not nurture the foundational skills needed for future literacy. "Educators sometimes conclude that phonemes must be taught to preschoolers only in an academic context with quizzing and work sheets. We've seen before that there are direct and indirect ways to teach young children preacademic skills, and those children most at risk for reading problems are usually ones in classrooms where they receive phonemic knowledge from a top-down, teacher-driven script" (Christakis, 2016).

Instead of activities involving rote memorization, let children play, a lot! Child-led play will develop phonological awareness skills and give children the strong foundations needed for phonics and reading instruction in elementary school. This will not leave them behind but rather, will sufficiently prepare them for literacy instruction when the time is right.

Why do these experiences work?

Before children can read or write, they must develop phonological awareness. Before they can identify the sounds letters make, their brains must be able to hear and isolate phonemes. These abilities develop when children experience an abundance of language in meaningful contexts. Predetermined curriculums with scripted teacher activities do not provide this, but child-led play does. Immersing children in environments rich with sounds, and encouraging them to converse with their peers are excellent ways to develop phonological awareness. These interactions build pathways in the brain needed to decipher and dissect the sounds of language.

WHOLE CHILD ALPHABET

CHAPTER FIVE

Writing the Alphabet Begins with Physical Development

"By nature's design, kids are born to move" (Connell & McCarthy, 2014). Let's go back to our childhoods. Remember seeing a tree and feeling the need to climb it? Seeing a hill, and wanting to roll down it? What about climbing to the top of the monkey bars, and hanging upside down? And swings! I remember trying my best to swing as high as possible and jump as far as I could, when dismounting. We took physical risks all the time with the goal of exceeding what we could do yesterday. We felt capable and accomplished. Did adults tell us to do this? No, it was intrinsically motivated. Our brains told our bodies we needed that movement for physical development and thankfully, many of us had opportunities to follow through and move as necessary. How amazing it was!

Physical Development, the Forgotten Domain

Focusing too much on kindergarten and school readiness diminishes what is important in the early years; especially physical development because it's not always connected to the "academic success" realm. This is a disservice to children. Physical development is as important as any other area when supporting the whole child. Physical development is just as critical for children achieving life success as the cognitive, language, and social/emotional domains. "The more closely we consider the elaborate interplay of brain and body, the more clearly one compelling theme emerges: movement is essential to learning and to the manifestation of life itself" (Hannaford, 2005).

A personal journey

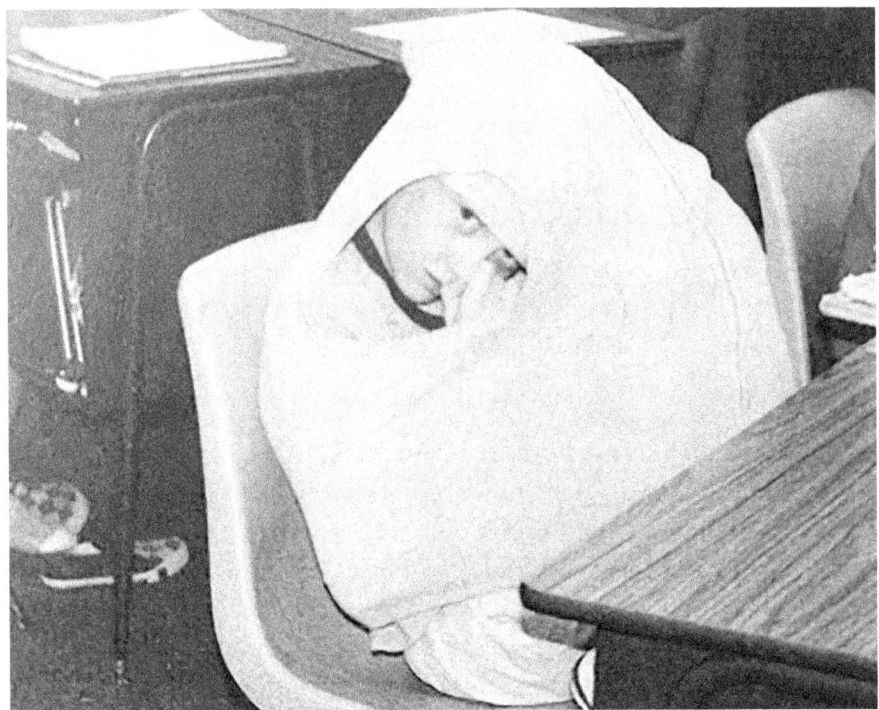

This picture of my oldest son Mason was taken when he was in the fourth grade. His teacher, who was phenomenal, sent this to me with a note saying, "This is how your son learns best." Mason struggled in school, and we were searching for ways to help him. How incredible that his teacher didn't reprimand him for sitting like this but recognized he was compensating to overcome some sort of challenge. Little did we know that this picture was a key to uncovering some of his struggles.

I took Mason to an occupational therapist for an evaluation. The results showed his torso, abs, and back were weak. His hamstrings were too tight which made it difficult for him to sit comfortably. In addition to this, his vestibular and proprioceptive systems were underdeveloped for his age. He also struggled with his visual perceptual skills which made it difficult for him to decipher what his eyes were seeing. Needless to say, he did not have the adequate physical skills to be successful in a classroom.

Looking at the picture, you can see how he figured out how to sit and learn in class. He requested to wear that same vest every day to school, and not as a fashion statement, but as a mechanism to help him function. He had to pull his legs up close to his body because the tight hamstrings caused severe discomfort when sitting. This, coupled with his weak core and vestibular system, meant that he needed his vest to keep his legs secure and his body steady in the chair. Pulling the vest over his head blocked out the visual stimuli he found distracting, but the arm hole provided enough of an opening for him to see and hear what was necessary. This took a lot of thought on his part. As the occupational therapist said, "How can he learn in school when all of his intelligence is being wasted on figuring out compensatory strategies?"

From ages 10 to 14, Mason spent hours every week going to occupational and physical therapy in addition to doing exercises daily at home. In essence, the therapists started at ground zero and "redesigned" his body. When I took Mason to his sessions, not only did I gain information about my son, but I used these opportunities to learn about the intricacies of physical development from the experts. There is a process to how the body grows and develops and it is important to honor that and not skip steps. The entire body works as a team and if one part is not fully developed, it can affect the functioning of the rest.

It is no surprise as Mason's body strengthened, his school performance vastly improved. He was able to pay attention to his teachers instead of worrying about how he was going to stay in his chair. Although we were thrilled with my son's progress at school, the therapists kept telling us all the effort transcended academics. A fully developed and functioning body affects a person's entire life. Because of this, I am passionate about physical development and respecting the developmental processes when it comes to motor skills. Yet another reason I advocate for children to have abundant opportunities to play and move around!

The Starting Point for Alphabet Writing

What does this have to do with alphabet knowledge? If there is an expectation from stakeholders for children to write before kindergarten, it is vital to understand the foundations needed for that task. Handwriting is a complex skill that requires more than placing a pencil in a child's hand and "teaching" them how to form the letters. Writing requires the entire body. Yes, the fine motor skills are important, but the performance of the small muscle movements rely heavily on the gross motor muscles being developed and stabilized. It is critical to respect the continuum of physical development and not skip steps. This is why I say, handwriting begins on the playground! So, instead of using curriculums that "teach" handwriting, take children outside and let them run around, climb, and play as much as possible.

Components of Physical Development

Let's look more closely at the progression of physical development. At infancy, this begins at the head then works its way down through the limbs. This includes the muscles strengthening, the internal senses developing, and the brain and body learning to work as a team. Because of this, we must design environments that allow plenty of time for children to play and move whenever needed.

Cephalocaudal/Proximodistal

The principles of cephalocaudal and proximodistal are important in understanding the sequence of physical development that goes from the top of the head down to the toes and also starts at the center of the body and progresses out to the fingers. Let's take a closer look at these concepts.

Cephalocaudal

Cephalocaudal means top down; development starts with the head and works its way down to the toes. Think of when a baby is born. Their head is the biggest part of their body, and we support it when holding them because their necks don't have the ability to do so. Eventually, their necks strengthen and they can start to hold up their head on their own. As we put babies on their tummies (when they are awake and fully supervised) they start to push up, engaging their torsos and upper backs. Eventually, they start to sit up using their abdominal muscles. Babies will start to get on all fours and rock back and forth and ultimately crawl, showing the progression moving into the legs. They then start to pull up and stand and, at around 12 months old, they start to walk. So, within one year's time, babies go from having all their movement dependent upon another person's support, to the ability to walk around on their own. It is remarkable how much physical development occurs in the first year of life.

Although a child can typically walk around one year of age, that doesn't mean their walking skills are refined. It takes time. Think of being at a soccer field or a dance recital. The kicks and shuffles of the younger children hinge from their hips. As the they get older, the actions originate more from their knees. By the time they are teenagers, the kicks and shuffles become more intricate, and the movements are more in their ankles, feet, and toes.

Proximodistal

Proximodistal means from the middle, out. This begins with the neck, torso, and back being developed and stabilized. The development then goes to the shoulders then travels down the arms stabilizing the elbows, wrists, hands, then the fingers. Let's reverse this to understand how the entire body supports handwriting. For the fingers to function and work in isolation, they rely on the development and stability of the hand. The hand depends on the development and stability of the wrist. The wrist hinges on the development and stability of the elbow. The elbow relies on the development and stability of the shoulder which bears the weight of the entire arm. And the shoulder depends on the development and stability of the neck, torso, and back. "This order of priority, established by the brain, ensures the large muscles necessary for coordination and locomotion are well developed first" (Connell & McCarthy, 2014). This is why it is difficult to isolate fine motor skills without regarding the importance of gross motor development.

Mobility on Stability

In addition to understanding how the body develops, it is important to recognize how the muscles support one another. "By nature's design, this logical progression ensures the larger muscles are ready to support and transport smaller muscles for more refined, detailed activity" (Connell & McCarthy, 2014). For the limbs to function, they must have a stable base, a concept known as proximal stability for distal mobility. This means the core must be developed and stabilized to support the movement of the arms and legs. Then, think of a succession down the limbs where the bigger muscles stabilize and support the mobility and function of the smaller ones. A stable shoulder supports the movement of the arm. A stable arm supports the mobility of the hands and fingers. It would be difficult to write if the arm was weak and limp and provided no support to the hand. This is the reason handwriting goes beyond just fine motor skills; we have to give credit where it is due for the role gross motor development plays in the process. Understanding this helps us advocate for outdoor play and big body movement as essential for children to eventually be able to write.

Fine Motor Development

All elements of physical development are interconnected; the whole body works together as a team to support any mobile function, including those of the fine motor muscles in the wrists, hands, and fingers. "There is a natural order to body control and the larger muscles need to be well developed before they can support the complexities of the many smaller muscles, bones, ligaments, and tendons of the hands" (O'Connor & Daly, 2016). Before focusing on fine motor activities, it is important to see how children's hands and fingers develop.

Separation of the hands
Early on, children use their hands as a whole, much like animals use their paws. Overtime, they develop what is considered separation of the hands. To visualize this, draw an imaginary line down your palm between your middle and ring fingers; this creates two sides of the hand with the thumb, index, and middle fingers on one side and the ring and pinky fingers on the other. When this emerges, children start to use the two parts of the hand separately to complete small motor tasks such as cutting with scissors and holding a pencil with an efficient grip.

It is important to recognize that this is a developmental process that needs to occur before children can successfully attempt certain fine motor tasks. It is not a matter of teaching; rather, it is a matter of developing. In other words, if a pencil is put in a child's hand before this emerges, they cannot be expected to hold it properly just because their fingers are "placed" in the correct position. If they don't have the ability, they cannot be taught; yet another reason to respect the nature of fine motor development. Instead of rushing to attain end goals, provide opportunities for children to play and develop separation of hand.

Fine motor strength
"The hands alone have more than 60 muscles, dozens of bones, and hundreds of ligaments and tendons" (Connell & McCarthy, 2014). The hands are intricate and have numerous working parts. Like every other part of the body, children must build strength in their fine motor muscles to perform everyday functions such as holding crayons to write and self-help skills including fastening buttons and zippers. This is achieved when children have plenty of hands-on opportunities to play with and manipulate real, three-dimensional objects.

Crossing the Midline

Midlines are known as the pivot points of the body. Looking at a person, their body can be divided three different ways: left and right, top and bottom, and front and back. Crossing midlines pertains to moving body parts to the opposite side of the body; such as moving the right arm over to the left side of the body. To perform everyday tasks, the ability to cross midlines must exist. Think about how many times a day you cross a midline. Reaching across the body to pick up a block. Bending down to tie a shoe. Moving a leg forward to take steps to walk. Even reading and writing requires the eyes and hands to cross left to right. When this happens, it indicates that the left and right sides of the brain are communicating and working together.

Midline Development

How does the ability to cross midlines develop? Through lots and lots of movement and play. The brain and body must have plenty of practice to learn to work as a team. When children have ample opportunities to move and naturally cross midlines, they build neurological pathways between the brain's left and right hemispheres which allow for efficient communication between the two. "In other words, midline development is essential to optimizing the 'whole brain'" (Connell & McCarthy, 2014).

Bilateral coordination

Bilateral coordination is the left and right sides of the body working together at the same time to perform a task. Bilateral movements may be mirrored, alternating, or different body parts moving independently, yet working in coordination together. With movement opportunities, children progress through the various stages of bilateral coordination.

- **Symmetrical**
  Symmetrical movement is a child moving both sides of the body at the same time to complete the same task. Imagine a baby raising both their left and right arms simultaneously to reach and grab a toy.

- **Reciprocal**
  Reciprocal movement is different sides of the body moving opposite one another. Walking and crawling are examples of this movement.

- **Asymmetrical**
  Asymmetrical movement is when the sides of the body engage in different motions but work to complete the same task. This includes holding a piece of paper with one hand as the other hand writes. Another example is one hand holding the bottom of a jacket while the other zips it up.

The significance of crossing midlines

As the left and right hemispheres start working together, the brain develops the ability to isolate body parts for independent movements and coordinated actions with other body parts. This is not only important for everyday tasks but for literacy as well. Think specifically of handwriting. Although other body parts participate, the arm and hand sweep from the left side of the paper to the right. No matter which hand is dominant, it will be crossing the body at some point. Consider crossing the midlines when reading. The eyes also move left to right to follow the text. One hand holds the book while the other turns the pages, crossing the body's midline right to left. Without a doubt, crossing midlines supports the coordination needed for the body to support literacy.

Midlines and the dominant hand

"Complex systems require organization, specialization, and leadership to streamline activity, avoid confusion, and produce the best results. And that goes for the human mind and body as well. That's why during the years of midline development, handedness emerges" (Connell & McCarthy, 2014).

The dominant hand struggles to develop if a child cannot cross midline. If a child is using both hands on their respective sides of the body, they are being used equally and neither have the opportunity to strengthen and dominate. If the child is crossing the midline, one hand tends to take over and become dominant. "As kids develop the ability to cross midline, they begin to feel one hand becoming stronger than the other when performing fine motor tasks. This will become their dominant hand" (Heffron, 2015). When this happens, the brain streamlines communication to one hand to complete the task instead of sending messages to both sides. This results in a more timely and efficient response. But this cannot happen unless children move and play and develop the ability to cross midlines.

Internal Sensory Development

When listing the senses, we typically include the abilities to see, hear, smell, taste, and touch. But there are internal senses as well that help keep the body in check and aware of what it is doing. These senses assist with everyday tasks, including reading and writing.

Vestibular

"Any kindergarten teacher will tell you that the three most important elements of school readiness are the abilities to sit still, pay attention, and stay focused. The vestibular system governs all three" (Connell & McCarthy, 2014). If the vestibular system is out of whack, it would be impossible to concentrate on anything other than staying stable. This is because the vestibular system helps maintain balance, posture, and orientation in space. Essentially, this is what keeps us upright and prevents us from falling over when standing or sitting. With this developed and intact, a person is more apt to be stable and focused.

The vestibular system consists of fluid stimulating little hairs in the inner ears which send information to the brain about where the body is in space and what is needed to maintain balance. This system works together with the visual system to provide information about the quality and direction of movement, and assists with connecting to the environment and moving about the surroundings. The sense of balance holds the head, eyes, and hands steady, which is important for literacy. Thanks to the vestibular system, the eyes have the ability to stay on the same line when reading, then steadily move to the next line of text. This sense also helps the hand keep the pencil on the line when writing, while maintaining consistent sizing of letters and adequate spacing between them.

It would be difficult to operate in everyday life without the development of the vestibular system. "When children have had insufficient experiences for their body to be well balanced, they will need to think and concentrate on maintaining balance and uprightness; their bodies are not yet mind-free, and this can inhibit focusing on and attending to other things" (Neaum, 2017). A child cannot sit in a classroom and learn if their vestibular system is underdeveloped. A child cannot read and write if they have not had adequate opportunities to develop their sense of balance. This is why it is important to understand the intricacies of child development and what needs to be in place before children can achieve the "academics" we expect from them. The vestibular system is the core of everything we do.

Proprioception

The proprioceptive system helps the brain know where the body is in space and how much strength is needed for a task. "Proprioception comprises sensory receptors in the joints, muscles, ligaments, and connective tissues that tell you where your body parts are without you having to look at them" (Hanscom, 2016). These receptors relay to the brain how the body parts are working together as well as the timing and force required of the muscles. This information helps the body maneuver and navigate the environment. In other words, you don't have to think of where to place your body when you sit or how much force is needed when picking up your phone, your proprioception takes care of that for you.

As an everyday example, think of going to the refrigerator and grabbing a gallon of milk. Without much thought, we, as adults, have enough life experience that our brains and bodies know how much strength is needed to pick up that gallon of milk, based on whether it is full, empty, or somewhere in between. That is our proprioceptive system working for us. But what happens if you think the gallon is full, but it is indeed empty? You grab the jug, and it goes flying! The same thing happens if you go to grab a box you think is heavy, but it is light. You use too much force. In these cases, the proprioceptive system is working, but the object deceived us.

How does this translate into literacy? There are a lot of things our bodies do when reading and writing that we don't give much thought to, because the proprioceptive system takes care of it. This sense aids in holding and manipulating books. When turning pages, it helps the fingers know how much pressure to use, to not tear the paper. (One of the reasons it is important to give children books with real pages is so they can learn this process. Pages will be unintentionally ripped, but children can't learn to regulate this unless they have some experience with it.) This internal sense also gives information about how much force to use when holding a pencil and how much pressure to put on the paper when writing. Even knowing where to place the hand on a page and the spatial orientation of writing letters depends on the proprioceptive system.

Developing Internal Senses

When studying the internal senses and understanding how they assist a person in everyday life, it is easy to see the importance of fully developing these systems. Like everything else mentioned, there is a starting point to their development, and it takes time, as well as experiences, for them to grow and mature. How does that happen? Much like a muscle, if the vestibular and proprioceptive systems are not engaged and challenged, they will not grow and develop. Children must constantly utilize these senses and find opportunities to challenge them with tasks a little bit or a lot harder than what they experienced yesterday. This is why movement is crucial to children's development. Climbing and hanging upside down! Spinning, swinging, sliding, and rolling! Running, walking, and crawling! Anything that puts the body and head in different positions to engage these systems, will help them develop. Children need to be freely moving about the room and the playground over and over again.

The best way to design an environment that allows for child-led movement is to encourage lots and lots of play! Design the environment, allow the movement, and step back and let children move. "Being in charge of their own vestibular stimulation is important as it means an activity is perfectly tuned to their individual stage of development" (O'Connor & Daly, 2016). This goes for the proprioceptive system too. Allowing children to control their movements is the best thing we can do. So, let's put child-led play on our lesson plans and let children move about as much as they need. We will only be setting them up for success.

Children's brains tell their bodies what they need, their bodies tell us

"Due to the lack of efficient movement opportunities today, many children walk around with an underdeveloped vestibular sense. The results: fidgeting, tears of frustration, more falls, aggression, and trouble with attention" (Hanscom, 2016). We prevent many of these movement opportunities in the name of safety or, for the sake of spending more time on getting children "ready for school." The result? Children may be stagnant or not moving as much as they should. If they are sitting still all the time, they are not developing the vestibular and proprioceptive systems, resulting in difficulties in school and life. If they are always following movements the adults have chosen, they are not getting the movement their individual bodies need. Remember, children's brains tell their bodies what they need, and their bodies tell us. So, if we see children fidgeting, moving, spinning and trying to climb or hang upside down, there's a reason for that. When we see children engaging in heavy work, such as carrying boxes full of blocks around the room as toddlers tend to do, there is a need. They're responding to their brain saying, "I need you to get up and move so we can develop these systems." Our role in this is to respect their cues and let them move as they see fit.

Coordination and Endurance

The brain and body working as a team to smoothly perform tasks is coordination. "Gross motor coordination is the ability to repeatedly execute a sequence of movements with accuracy and precision" (Hanscom, 2016). Coordination relies on the development of the body, crossing midlines, and the internal senses. All these mechanisms work together to effortlessly move the body about in everyday life. Add endurance, the ability to stick with something before tiring out, and you have the necessary components which ensure the body is able to complete the task at hand.

Physical Development and Alphabet Knowledge

The existence of the alphabet is dependent upon print. Learning how to form and utilize the letters for communication relies on handwriting. Numerous curriculums focusing on the alphabet have a writing component; unfortunately, many of them are in the form of traceable worksheets. Yes, learning how to correctly form the letters is important, but before children can trace worksheets, they must be physically and developmentally ready for the task. Not just their hands, but their entire bodies.

Handwriting

"The highest-level skill humans perform with their hands is handwriting. Children have the most success with learning how to write when their hands are appropriately developed [and] their brains are cognitively ready to receive instruction in writing (which is usually between kindergarten and 1st grade) ..." (Gibbs, 2015). Do you remember your first experience with formal handwriting instruction? For me, it was in the first grade when my teacher had us go to the chalk board (a vertical surface) and make straight lines down. In fact, in talking with many of my friends, this seems to be the consensus for most who started school before 1980. It was a simple starting point, but it aligned with our capabilities. I don't remember any traceable worksheets until well into that school year when most of us were turning seven years old. There was wisdom in the approach my first-grade teacher took.

"Children who write before they are developmentally ready may experience undesirable outcomes such as poor pencil grasp and letter formation habits that are difficult to change" (Gibbs, 2015). The lines are getting blurred between basic development and developmental delays when it comes to handwriting. The unfounded expectation that children should be correctly forming letters before entering kindergarten has resulted in a skewed perception that if they are not doing this, they are behind. The reality is, young children's bodies are not developmentally ready for formal handwriting; not because they are delayed, but because they are naturally developing children, progressing through the developmental stages as they should. Just because we want children to start writing early doesn't mean they are ready to do so. Handwriting is a matter of developing, not teaching. Absolutely, correct letter formation is a taught skill, but its success depends on adequate physical development. Let's respect that.

It is important to remember that handwriting is a complex process that requires the coordination of multiple body parts interdepedently working to support moving a pencil about the paper. Fine motor skills are important, but they rely on the entire body being fully developed and stabilized. Dr. Marianne Gibbs lists the following prerequisites to handwriting in her book *Fine Motor Skills... Write Out of the Box!: A Guide to Fine Motor Development for the Whole Child*. (2015)

- Established hand dominance (usually emerges between 4.5 – 6 years old)

- Ability to cross the midline

- Ability to use two hands in an activity (asymmetrical bilateral movements)

- Ability to coordinate eyes and hands together (eye-hand coordination)

- Functional pencil grasp ("Acquisition of an efficient pencil grasp is a process pattern development that usually settles in later between 4.5 and 6 years old for typically developing children" (Gibbs, 2015).)

- Recognition of similarities and difference in forms (visual discrimination)

- Ability to understand directional terms

- Orientation to print

- Recognition of letter forms and sounds (letter recognition and phonemic awareness)

- Ability to copy basic shapes: vertical line, horizontal line, circle, plus sign, slanted lines (forward and backward), square with defined sides, X, triangle with defined corners

- Ability to maintain proper sitting posture (core strength)

- Interest in handwriting

- Ability to attend to a task for a minimum of one minute (for purposes of receiving formal instruction in handwriting)

What do we do about handwriting?

It is possible to teach children to format letters while respecting their stage of physical development. This is done by providing opportunities for children to see how to form letters in a meaningful context without giving them traceable worksheets. By doing that, and focusing on stable physical development, children will be ready to practice handwriting when it is developmentally appropriate for them.

We created the market for handwriting curriculums

"Pre-K children are not ready for either formal paper/ pencil lessons or for kindergarten workbooks" (Olsen & Knapton, 2016). I once attended a training on a widely used handwriting curriculum. They stated that children shouldn't be introduced to formal handwriting instruction at a young age, but since we [the early childhood community] were going to force it anyway, they might as well give us some guidance. We created the market for handwriting curriculum (and really any curriculum) with our fear of children being behind, and not ready for school. Then we justify inappropriate practices by pointing to the "requirements" of a curriculum, and state either "they know better than us" or "the approach is out of our hands." (And in all fairness, sometimes the curriculums are used incorrectly.)

Predetermined curriculums are not responsible for our learning environments, we are. It is our responsibility to move past the school readiness mentality and focus back on the whole child. This shifts the mindset to child development and designing an environment that supports that through play. We can probably implement a few elements of the curriculum too, but not let it dictate everything that is done in the setting. It is important to use good professional judgment and recognize when a required curriculum or some aspect of it does not align with our beliefs. As a profession, we need to stand in our convictions of what we know as right and stop sacrificing healthy child development for the sake of school readiness.

Why is this information important?

"Children regularly show us what they are capable of and what they need and benefit from. If they are constantly moving, and physically challenging themselves in new ways, it must be fundamental to their lives" (Curtis, 2018). Physical development is essential for everyday functioning and affects school performance just as much as any of the other domains. Physical development means children rolling, spinning, jumping, running, twisting, bending, wiggling, and shaking all the time! Part of helping adults understand this is knowing that the whole child is a complex system, and that the brain and body learn to work as a team through child-led movement. It is also understanding the pattern in which gross and fine motor skills develop and support one another. Being able to verbalize all of this is critical in our stakeholder conversations as it explains the importance of play and children guiding their own movements. It also helps us clarify why sitting still and following adult driven activities is not in the best interest of physical development. This is the pillar we need, to advocate for child-led play in our settings.

CHAPTER FIVE

Experiences to Promote Physical Development

"Children literally thrive by challenging their bodies" (Hanscom, 2016). For children to develop physically, learning environments must be created that invite and encourage lots of movement, including big body movement, and opportunities to repeat movements if the child chooses. If children do not have the chance to challenge their bodies, they will not develop. Let's look at environments and experiences designed to strengthen physical development.

The experiences portion is divided into two sections. The first provides experiences that promote physical development, the second offers experiences that support letter formation.

Ensure proper supervision and compliance with all regulating agencies when selecting activities. Follow children's cues and let them participate in a manner that is comfortable for them.

Movements to Encourage All Day, Every Day

The following are movements that engage the neck, torso, shoulders, elbows, wrists, and hands. They also encourage crossing midlines and developing the internal senses by engaging the receptors in the inner ears as well as in the joints and muscles. Although the goal of this section is to highlight different movements and positions children may engage in while playing, these activities can also be included during group times, music and movement activities, and transition times.

Tummy time
Tummy time is essential in developing the torso and the core, but it is not just for babies; tummy time should be for all ages! When we design an environment that allows children to freely play, they naturally end up in positions on their tummies, propped up on their forearms, and crossing their midlines by reaching and gathering materials. At group time, instead of sitting crisscross applesauce, let children lie on their stomachs and prop up on their forearms and look at you or the book you are sharing. This is another great way to engage the neck, shoulders, torso, and back!

Superhero/ Ball Up
Superhero and ball ups can occur naturally or can be implemented into group time experiences. Superhero is lying on the tummy and lifting the torso and arms up off the ground along with the legs either alternately or at the same time. Lift them up and flutter the arms and legs and pretend to swim in the air! Ball Up is lying down on the back with arms and legs outstretched on the ground. The next step is to tuck the arms and legs in, to create a ball. This is a great position to roll back and forth or side to side. All of these movements are great for back and stomach muscles as well as engaging the neck, torso, and shoulders.

Crawling and Rocking on All Fours
"The crawling position on the hands and knees strengthens shoulder and hip muscles and, although probably wobbly at first, helps body awareness and the beginning of a sense of upright balance" (O'Connor & Daly, 2016). Think of how crawling engages the brain to move each side of the body in opposition, crossing the midlines with a reciprocal movement. Although we associate crawling with older infants, it is important for physical development of older children too as it engages the upper part of the body. Another example of child-led play providing what children need most - think of how many times crawling occurs naturally when children are on the floor playing!

Bear Crawl, Hermit Crab Walk, and Body Bridges
Bear crawling, hermit crab walking, and body bridges all put the body's weight on the hands and feet. All these positions require the shoulders to hold the body up, in addition to engaging core strength. These movements also put the head in various positions which develops the vestibular systems, while the joints supporting the body weight helps with proprioception.

To bear crawl, bend forward and walk on your feet and hands. Suspending the knees ensures the body is being held up by only the hands and feet. Move about the room, under tables, or down the hallway!

The hermit crab walk is almost the opposite of a bear crawl. Start by sitting on the floor then place the hands and feet on the ground and push the rest of the body up off the floor. Like the bear crawl, use the hands and feet to move about the space.

A body bridge is either of those positions, but staying stationary. Child-led play provides plenty of opportunities for children to naturally create this position.

(Think of using the body to make a bridge over a train track.) Again, these are wonderful for engagement of neck, shoulders and wrists, as well as the internal senses.

Hand presses

Hand presses involve the body's weight being placed on the hands, engaging the wrists and shoulders. This occurs naturally when crawling, pressing on playdough, and climbing. While waiting outside the bathroom during my time as a teacher, the children and I would do wall pushups (they decided individually how many to do for what best suited their abilities) which was a fun way to spend the time and a great opportunity for hand presses.

Heavy work

"To maintain and strengthen the proprioceptive system, encourage your child to have play experiences that offer resistance to the joints, muscles, and connective tissues. This can also be referred to as doing "heavy work," which basically consists of activities that require pushing, pulling, and carrying heavy objects" (Hanscom, 2016). If the environment is intentionally designed, heavy work occurs naturally. Climbing and pulling the body weight on the playground equipment outside, digging in the sand box, building with big, wooden blocks, filling containers and roaming around the room with them and dumping the contents someplace else – all of these activities will naturally emerge during child-led play. What better way to engage the proprioceptive system than to walk around with a heavy container, then dump it out to feel something light? And yes, children will repeat these actions because their brains are encouraging them to build their muscles and internal senses. Think of all the connections the brain and body are making during these simple experiences.

> ### *Filling and dumping*
>
> If you work with toddlers and twos, you know one of their favorite things to do is fill a container of any kind, walk around the room with it, then dump all the contents out on the floor. Don't battle it, just embrace it. Why? You guessed it – children's brains tell their bodies what they need, and their bodies respond.
>
> Although this is development at its best, it does create a messy room. That is okay, because toddlers and twos love to fill! If the mess gets out of control, sit on the floor with a container and start filling it with the materials strewn across the floor. Say, "I am going to fill this box with blocks. Who would like to join me?" Most of the time, they will jump at the opportunity to fill something up. Will the mess

reoccur soon after cleaning? You bet! Because this is what toddlers' and twos' brains are telling them to do.

One more thing, if a stakeholder walks in and asks about the mess, reassure them that it is intentional, and children are developing their gross and fine motor skills, vestibular and proprioceptive senses, spatial awareness, and volumetric reasoning (understanding full, then empty). Explain why you are letting it happen over and over and why it is essential to development.

Running, Galloping, Skipping, Leaping, Marching, Stomping, Hopping, and Jumping

When we engage in these movement experiences, our bodies are going against gravity, creating another form of heavy work. This allows the body weight to engage the receptors in the muscles and joints that then report back to the brain. These experiences also engage the vestibular system and encourage the body to cross midlines. Of course, we can implement these movements into a group time experience, but how can we create an environment that encourages this during play time? Provide plenty of space that lets children move as needed. If possible, encourage them to go uphill, backwards, and on uneven surfaces such as sand and gravel to further engage the internal senses and the core.

Rolling and Spinning

The internal senses cannot develop without being challenged; the vestibular system cannot learn to overcome dizziness unless it gets the chance to practice. So, let's get dizzy! This also helps with body awareness and establishing the center and the core. A great way for children to do this is spinning and rolling. "Spinning in circles is one of the best activities to help children gain a good sense of body awareness" (Hanscom, 2016). We can provide opportunities for rolling and spinning during music and movement or transitions, but what about during child-led play? Provide space and materials that promote these types of movements. Perhaps it's as simple as holding scarves and twirling around with them. You could use wedge mats which children can roll down, or scooter boards to sit on and spin. Maybe it is letting children twist up the swing and spin around. Whatever it is, find ways to let children roll, spin, and do any other type of movement that challenges their sense of balance.

Climbing

Children need to climb. If their environments won't allow it, they will be left to their own devices to find a way to do it. This is why many children climb the furniture in the room. They are honestly responding to their bodies telling them what they need to develop their own internal senses. Climbing engages the torso and the shoulders as well as the hands as they are gripping and helping pull the body. So, let's create environments inside and outside that encourage climbing. Find ways to provide climbing structures in the classroom so the opportunity is always there. Evaluate the playground equipment to ensure it invites and allows climbing. (Check with your local licensing agency on guidance for fall zones and appropriate ground coverings.) What about climbing up the slide? "Letting kids climb up slides… is a great way to help them strengthen their upper body and improve motor control" (Hanscom, 2016). Children usually prefer going up the slide anyway, so why don't we find a way to give them permission to do so? If this is something that's not permitted within your organization, get the conversation going with stakeholders on how this can be allowed.

Hanging upside down

"By changing directions and position of the head, children activate different parts of the brain" (Hanscom, 2016). This may rock the boat, but children need to hang upside down. Moving the head around stimulates the fluid in the inner ear that helps engage the vestibular system and develop spatial awareness. Hanging upside down on playground equipment, like many of us did as children, is a great way to do it. As always, discuss with licensing agents to see if your rules permit this activity. (Many times our assumptions of what may or may not be allowed are not accurate, so actually have the conversation.) Find other ways for children to put their heads in different positions. Let children tumble when on the playground. Incorporate yoga and stretching. Possibly provide thick mats (about 1 foot thick) in the environment where children can recline and hang their heads off the side. (Think of hanging your head off the couch when you were little.) Whatever it may be, explore ways to allow children to experience hanging upside down.

Materials for Play Environments

Here are some possible materials to include in the learning environment that promote movement and support physical development.

The floor!

One of the best things for physical development is being on the floor, moving around and playing. Children need lots of time on the floor. "The floor is a child's first, best playground – an experimental laboratory for learning, even from the youngest age" (Connell & McCarthy, 2014). We contain children too much. As infants and toddlers, we keep them in holding devices -- bouncy seats, floor seats, exercise saucers, tables with bucket seats, etc. While this might make the adults' lives easier, it isn't ideal for children's physical development. For preschool children, we keep them sitting in group times or in their chairs at tables for periods of time. This is not ideal for developing the body. Think of the movements mentioned in the last section and how many of them can naturally occur if children are allowed to be on the floor playing. That is where they need to be.

Easels and vertical surfaces

Grab a pencil and write on a piece of paper on a desk or table. Now hold the pencil in the air and pretend to write. Feel the difference with your shoulder? Lifting the arm up to a vertical surface engages and strengthens the shoulder. Easels are a wonderful way to provide this opportunity. If there is not enough space in the classroom, tape big pieces of paper on the wall for drawing and writing. Another option is to tape the paper under a table and have children lie down and extend their arms to draw. Go outside and paint the side of the building with water and paint brushes. Finger plays also invite children to hold their arms up, which also engages the shoulders.

Hands-on materials

Children need hands-on experiences to develop not only fine motor skills, but eye-hand coordination as well. Place various materials of different weights, textures, and sizes in the setting and invite children to freely play with them. This is one of the best ways to get the hands ready for writing and small motor tasks. These materials also assist in the development of the internal senses and the midlines. The following are some hands-on materials to consider.

- Sensory tables for digging, pouring, and sifting
- Blocks and building materials
- Small world manipulatives including people, furniture, and vehicles
- Finger puppets
- Dramatic play props
- Tennis and plastic balls
- Sensory balls
- Lacing cards and beads

- Pegs and pegboards
- Playdough
- Paper for crumpling, tearing, and folding
- Crayons, pencils, and chalk (they require more effort and strength than markers)
- Scissors and glue
- Squeeze toys
- Squirt bottles
- Turkey basters
- Eye droppers
- Tweezers
- Tongs
- Clothespins

Gross motor materials

Fine motor skills hinge on gross motor development and stabilization. The learning environment needs to invite big body movements and not see this activity as rowdy play that disrupts learning. Provide materials that entice children to roll, spin, jump, and move around. Here are some ideas. (Again, if you think something is questionable or not allowed, have a conversation with your licensing agents and see what can be worked out.)

- Wedge mats for rolling and reclining in various positions
- Mats for cushion
- Low, foam, balance beam
- Foam stepping stones
- Crawl tunnels
- Scooter boards
- Wiggle/ balance discs
- Paper plates for skating
- Boxes, carts, or wheelbarrows for filling and moving
- Laundry baskets to fill and climb in
- Hula hoops

- Balls
- Bean bags
- Scarves and streamers
- Large sheets of paper on wall and floor for drawing

Outdoor learning environments

Between safety restrictions and maintenance, we have stripped playgrounds of the essential elements children truly need to take risks, grow, and develop. Many outdoor environments have become plastic and sterile. Although we tend to blame regulating agencies and licensing standards, we can also ask ourselves about the extent of conversation we've had with these authorities. I recently talked with an administrator who transformed the outdoor area at her school to a natural playscape. She assumed licensing would restrict all her ideas, but to her surprise, they didn't. Her assumptions of what wouldn't work based on her interpretations of the standards, were incorrect. Once she initiated the conversations with the licensing reps, she was amazed at how many of her ideas they allowed. The moral of the story? Get the conversation started. Talk with regulating agencies and specifically ask what is and is not allowed. If something is stated as not allowed, collaborate to find something that works within the realm of the regulations. These conversations might persuade others and lead to change.

"Modern playgrounds and play areas often provide a high level of safety but a low level of challenge" (Connell & McCarthy, 2014). In their book *A Moving Child is a Learning Child*, Gill Connell and Cheryl McCarthy suggest the following items to create a great playground.

- Hills
- Trees
- Modular elements (hoops, cones, blocks)
- Monkey bars
- Swings
- Merry-go-rounds
- Planks and beams
- Tunnels
- See-saw
- Slides

When designing the outdoor learning environment, consider the following items in addition to the ones listed above. For everything, check fall zones and provide appropriate ground coverings.

- Playground equipment that encourages all types of big body movement
- Space and opportunity to run, spin, and jump
- Uneven surfaces to engage the core
- Natural items
- Sand box and toys
- Water table and pouring stations
- Riding toys (wear helmets)
- Hopping ball or horse (wear helmets)
- Building materials
- Large loose parts
- Big cardboard boxes
- Different sized balls
- Easels and paint
- Small buckets, water, and paint brushes
- Sidewalk chalk

- **Risky play**
"Safety is important, opportunities for developmentally appropriate risk-taking are more so" (Murphy, 2020). Since children must challenge their bodies for development, they will seek risky play. Typically, they will push limits by climbing higher, jumping farther, and spinning faster. Without these movements, their muscles and internal systems will not adequately develop.

There are multiple benefits to children taking risks, including knowing how to handle their bodies and maneuver the environment. Preventing risky play may hinder their physical development. "Limiting children's exposure to risk and constantly trying to keep them from falling can impede their physical development" (Hanscom, 2016). Instead of restricting, we need to encourage the risks while at the same time removing the hazards. Figure 17 is a table that helps distinguish a risk from a hazard.

Figure 17

Risk	Hazard
Child chooses	Child not aware of
Outside comfort zone	Broken/ damaged equipment
Engage and challenge	Endangerment such as entrapment
Growth as a result	No benefits
Adults need to encourage	Adults need to eliminate

Success begins on the playground

"Safety is a myth: risk is a reality" (Nebelong, 2017). Not only is risk-taking necessary for physical development, it is an important part of overall human development. The child taking risks on the playground will one day become the adult stepping outside of their comfort zone to achieve something great. Whether it's applying for a promotion, setting a health and wellness goal, meeting new people or trying new things, taking risks is part of life. When the situation doesn't go as planned, we get up and try again; this is part of growing as a person. These life skills are practiced early on, when children take risks on the playground.

Group Time Experiences

These offerings could be used in group time with the entire class, or as a spontaneous group time with a few children if they show interest. However, please don't let them replace child-led play time. Engage in these activities during play time or outdoors and see who chooses to join in. Provide the materials for the children to engage with on their own as well.

Group time sitting

Speaking of group experiences, why do we insist on children sitting crisscross applesauce during group times? As adults, we move in our chairs and change positions when sitting for periods of time because the muscles become fatigued or even fall asleep. How would we feel if someone told us we must stay in the same position? It is the same for children. If they are fidgeting or trying to sit a different way, they need to for some reason. Why not let them? Let them lie on their stomachs or sides and prop themselves on their forearms. This engages the neck, torso, back, shoulders, and elbows. What about side sitting? A lot of times when side sitting, children shift the weight of their body to one side allowing them to naturally cross the midline. Sit with legs straight out front to lengthen the back of the legs. A child lying on their back and propping their upper body on forearms to see is engaging the upper body and the core.

No "W" sitting

One thing to avoid is the "W" sitting position. "'W' sitting occurs when children sit on the floor with their legs positioned in the shape of a 'W'... Children may develop a habit for 'W' sitting as a way to establish increased stability in their bodies when they cannot assume and maintain the crisscross (tailor) sitting position" (Gibbs, 2015). When children do this, they are creating a base with their legs to stabilize themselves instead of engaging the core to keep themselves upright. This position restricts trunk rotation and crossing the midlines as well. "This wide base also limits a child's need to weight shift on their bottom from side to side during play, resulting in decreased use of balance responses. This lack of activation causes a cycle of muscle weakness, resulting in difficulty integrating the left and right sides of the body, leading to decreased coordination. These impairments can lead to decreased play involving crossing over the body's midline and poor progress with high-level fine motor tasks using two hands." (Brown, n.d.) If you see children sitting this way, encourage them to switch to a different position.

Music and movement

All the movements and skills mentioned thus far can be practiced in music and movement time. When planning this as group time, be intentional and make sure the experiences meet the needs of the children and their physical development, and are not limited to weekly themes. Try different things, and find ways to get up and really move.

Yoga/stretching

Find opportunities to stretch and practice yoga. Think of doing this before read aloud or nap time as a great way to calm the mood, in addition to moving the body and crossing midlines. Although there are great opportunities to engage in these experiences during teacher-directed time, stretching the body can also happen naturally when children are playing and moving outside.

Big body experiences

The following experiences encompass big body movements. Many of them are variations of tabletop activities. The majority of these are teacher-directed, but children may engage in them on their own if they have access to the materials.

Sock Ball Throw

(A matching/ sorting activity with small manipulatives.)

Materials

Laundry baskets, random pairs of socks, and music

Activity

- Unfold socks and mix them all together
- Scatter socks around the room
- Play music and encourage children to dance
- Have each child pick up one sock and dance around the room waving it in the air
- Find the person dancing around with the matching sock
- Fold the socks together
- Dance over to the laundry basket to toss the pair of socks in
- Continue until all the socks are gathered and placed in the laundry baskets

Variations

- Label the laundry baskets for sorting (Color, Solid/ Patterns, Long/ Short)
- Use items other than socks (Pick paper off floor, crumple and throw in basket)

Mazes

Materials

Carpet squares

Activity

Line up carpet squares in the form of a maze

Have children walk/ hop/ crawl/ sidestep/ walk backwards on the squares

Variations

Create the maze using a variety of materials. (Unit blocks/ painter's tape/ ribbon)

Line chairs up to create a maze for children to crawl under

Create a maze outside using sidewalk chalk

Tie crepe paper to tables and chairs to climb over and under (ensure no hazards)

Play music and have children freeze on the maze when the music stops

Hot Lava
(Remember playing this as a child, jumping couch to couch?)

Materials

Carpet squares

Activity

Spread carpet squares across the room

Encourage children to jump square to square without stepping on the floor

Variations

Create boxes on floor with painter's tape if carpet squares slide too much on surface

Draw boxes outside with sidewalk chalk

Play music and have children freeze when the music stops

The Big Haul

(This experience will occur naturally if the materials are available for the children. It can be a group time experience as well.)

Materials

Laundry basket/ boxes

Materials with weight

Activity

Fill the container with something of weight

Encourage children to move the basket/ box around the room

Variations

Create a maze to move box around

Play music and have the children freeze when the music stops

Sheet Pull

(This experience will occur naturally if the materials are available for the children. It can be a group time experience as well.)

Materials

Twin sheet/ small blanket/ laundry basket

Big area with floor space inside or grassy area outside

Activity

Have one child sit on sheet and other children pull them around

Variations

Place cones to maneuver around

CHAPTER FIVE

Bear Hunt

("Going on a Bear Hunt" is typically done sitting in group time. Make it big instead!)

Activity

Move about the room while "swimming through the stream," "trudging through mud," and "galloping through tall grass"

Variations

Take this outside!

"But we have enrichment programs for that"

If your organization includes enrichment programs, great! Enrichment programs are supplements to what already exists in the learning environments, they are not replacements because they do not provide the sustenance of child-led play. Ideally, scheduling these programs would be child-centered, and would not disrupt or supercede meaningful play time. When planning the rest of the day, keep in mind that time spent in an adult-guided enrichment activity should be balanced with time in child-led play.

You might share this information with the instructor of the enrichment program, whether they are on staff or from an outside company, so they understand the importance of movement and can be intentional with their planning. Also ensure they understand that children's bodies respond to their brains, so they may seek experiences other than what is planned or on the curriculum. "As adults, we may feel that we always know what is best for our children. A child's neurological system begs to differ. Children with healthy neurological systems naturally seek out the sensory input they need on their own. They determine how much, how fast, and how high works for them at any given time. They do this without even thinking about it. If they are spinning in circles, it is because they need to. If they are jumping off a rock over and over, it is because they are craving sensory input. They are trying to organize their senses through practice and repetition" (Hanscom, 2016). Make sure the enrichment teachers know that it is okay to scrap the plan and follow the children's cues. The program is even more enriching when this happens!

Most importantly, enrichment programs do not take the place of movement in our learning environments. We cannot rely on a structured program to provide the movement while reserving the classrooms for "teaching." Physical movement should be an option at any moment in our settings. The opportunity for children to move their bodies as needed should always be allowed; in fact, encouraged. Children respond to how their brains are telling them to move, a pre-planned activity might not meet that need. Although many enrichment programs are designed to build gross and fine motor skills, they don't allow the opportunity for physical development like true, authentic play. Therefore, it is vital to provide big chunks of time for child-led play so children can move, and repeat the moves, as they see fit.

Experiences for Proper Letter Formation

You might be thinking, "We've been discussing physical development so much, but how do children learn to form the letters?" Seeing how letters are formed is critical in handwriting. The urge to make sure children know how to write the letters sometimes nudges us toward traceable worksheets. Resist that urge! Children can learn how to form letters without tracing dot-to-dot forms of them. Traceable worksheets are not developmentally appropriate, even if a prepackaged curriculum includes them. Use your professional judgement and discern what materials are best for young children.

"Although the preschool years are not the time for formal lessons in handwriting, teachers can assist children in ways that will help them develop some skill" (Schickedanz & Collins, 2013). Learning environments can provide opportunities for children to experience letter formation without paper and pencil. The following ideas and experiences need to connect to the child's world in order to resonate. Consider how you might incorporate these ideas naturally, in ways that connect to children's play.

Model Handwriting Frequently for Children

When I was little, I distinctly remember sitting and watching my mom write checks to pay the bills, and address the envelopes to mail them. Because of digital technology, writing in front of children is a lost art. Children see us typing into our phones and our computers, but they don't see us writing anymore. Children need to see adults write. Not only does it show them how to use written communication to function in the world, but this is one of the best ways to model proper letter formation. "The sequence and direction of drawing lines to form a letter cannot be discerned from looking at already formed letters nor easily grasped from worksheets with arrows and numbers marking lines in a model letter. The best learning comes from watching demonstrations" (Schickedanz & Collins, 2018). Find opportunities to write in the learning environment in contexts that are meaningful to children, and encourage families to do this as well.

CHAPTER FIVE

Move away from traceable worksheets

If I had my wish, all early care and education teachers would throw away their handwriting worksheets. It doesn't matter if a curriculum company designed them; I believe they have no place in an early childhood program. Handwriting worksheets tend to creep in when we believe that if we just introduce a skill earlier, children will learn it. Worksheets also feed into adults' fears of children being behind or not being ready for school. Learning to write is not a matter of teaching early, but rather, being patient and letting children adequately develop.

Handwriting is a complex task. Children's bodies need to reach a certain level of development before they can hold a pencil and trace letters. To give perspective on how introducing this too early might feel for children, find a traceable worksheet and a pencil. Place the pencil in your non-dominant hand (the hand you don't write with) and try tracing the worksheet. What do notice? You might have difficulty staying on the lines and you probably write more slowly, but what do you notice about your body? Are you pulling your shoulder up close to your ear? What about pulling the elbow up in the air? Feel like you might be doing a death grip on the pencil or holding it oddly with your fingers? It most likely feels awkward, clumsy, and uncomfortable. Why is this happening? I gave you a task your non-dominant arm does not quite have the ability to complete, so you are compensating by lifting your shoulder, raising your elbow, and holding the pencil too tight. We do the same thing to children when we introduce worksheets before their bodies are ready. You will most likely see them doing the same thing you did with your non-dominant arm. Remember, children's bodies tell us what they need. If children are raising shoulders and elbows, holding the pencil with a firm grip, and anything else peculiar with their bodies, they are sending an important message: they are compensating and compromising their proper physical development to attempt a task that is not developmentally appropriate. We need to listen to children and get traceable worksheets out of the setting.

Transcribe What Children Say

One of the most powerful connections for children when it comes to writing is to see their verbal words turn into print. Find lots of opportunities for children to tell you something and then write what they say. This can be done a variety of ways in both group time experiences and play times. As you model writing in front of children, spell the words verbally as you write, so children can see how each letter is formed.

Language charts
I asked the children in my class an open-ended question every week. Typical questions were:

- How do you make your favorite meal?

If you were the teacher, what would you do?

If you could travel anywhere, where would you go?

What is the most hilarious thing you have ever seen?

How do you fall asleep?

I would find a time throughout the week to individually ask each child the question without interrupting their play. (I did this individually instead of at group time so the children wouldn't copy each other's answers.) I had a big piece of paper and a bucket of markers. Each child picked the color of marker I used to write their answer. I asked the question, then I wrote the answer EXACTLY as they said it. I didn't change the tense, I didn't make it grammatically correct, I respected what the children said and wrote the same words they used. At the end of the week, once everyone responded, I read all the answers at group time, unless a child asked me not to. (I had some children who would get embarrassed if I read their statement out loud, so I respected that and skipped their answer.)

After reading to the group, I would post the answers outside the room for the families to read. After a year or two, I got smart and started typing the answers into an electronic document each week in addition to posting. At the end of the year, I printed a copy for each family, put it in a binder, and made an "end of the year" book. It progressed with the school year and was efficient, meaningful, and pleasing to families.

Open-ended scribbling and drawing

Embrace the power of blank paper and crayons! These are some of the most significant, essential tools to satisfy the desire to communicate messages through writing. Placing these throughout the learning environment allows children to freely express their thoughts on paper and share with others. This is how the writing process begins, connecting to children's worlds and allowing them to share what is meaningful to them.

Structuring a message requires symbolizing it utilizing either drawings, or letters and words. Writing composition is a developmental process that has a starting point. The evolution of writing begins with mark making, when young children experiment with making marks by either running their hands through water, food, or any other sensory substance. The ability to make marks is empowering and, if given the opportunity, children will continue with blank paper and crayons. This will begin as random scribbling, but with experience, will progress into scribbling with some control. Children will begin to repeat their scribbles and start to draw pictures that might resemble something in their worlds. About this time, a child might develop the ability to attribute meaning to what they have put on paper. Eventually, as the vocabulary increases, the stories become more elaborate, and children might need more than one piece of paper to adequately depict their story. As the drawings progress, letters of the alphabet will start to emerge on the paper. Over time, with ample opportunity for open-ended drawing and writing, children start to combine letters into letter strings. Couple this with the emergence of phonemic awareness, and children may begin to inventively spell words based on what they are hearing. A few years into elementary school, usually around the age of 8, conventional spelling is introduced, and children start to rely on words to share their messages instead of pictures.

- **Emerging letters**
  How does the writing composition process relate to alphabet knowledge and letter formation? One of the stages of writing is the emergence of letters next to children's drawings. This signifies children beginning to make the connection that letters serve a purpose in conveying a written message. Instead of being symbols that just float around the world for decoration, children begin to see letters as tools that are functional and represent something. This is an important part of alphabet knowledge. And what better way for children to make these connections than through experiences that are important to them and relate to their worlds? This is another reason to have blank paper and crayons throughout the setting so that children can draw and write about what connects to their ecosystems. And by the way, don't expect the first letter to emerge to relate to the drawing on the paper; chances are, the first letter to emerge will be the first letter of the child's first name, because that is the most important letter to them!

- **Not the time for worksheets**
  A critical note about letters emerging on open-ended drawings. Many times, when this happens, it is misinterpreted as the child being ready to trace and properly form the letters. They are appearing on the paper, so why not? It is important to understand that the emergence of letters means the child recognizes letters are purposeful and needed to convey a written message. This does not mean the child is physically ready for traceable worksheets. These are two totally separate processes, both important for writing, but composed of different skill sets.

Don't stop the process by teaching proper formation

You may ask, "If it is emerging on the paper, isn't this the right time to model the correct way to write it?" My answer is, does the situation naturally allow you to model the correct formation? In other words, has the child shared their drawing then asked you to write something on their paper? If so, this opens the door for you to subtly model the correct formation of the letter. But if the child is not asking us to do that, we should not constantly correct their attempts at writing. This will stifle the children's efforts and will discourage them playing around and attempting to write. Remember, this is a process that requires experience and child-led repetition. To keep it child-centered, let them be. Show an interest in what they are doing, and find other opportunities to naturally model the correct letter formation.

Transcribe the story

When a child shares their drawing, reply with, "Can you tell me about this?" My experience is most of the time if a child brings it to you, they want to engage in a conversation. The question gives them control of the situation. If they say yes, let them tell you all about it. (One of the most important roles educators play is being available for experiences such as this.) Then proceed to ask, "Do you want me to write what you're saying?" If they say yes, ask, "Do you want me to write this on your paper or on a separate sheet?" This is the child's creation; therefore, we may not write on their paper without their permission. (This includes their name.) If they give you permission to write on the paper, go for it. If not, have notecards or separate paper available to write on. Either way, write exactly what the child says, respecting their words and how they tell the story. Children seeing their spoken words written down is one of the most powerful connections for print awareness. It is also a perfect opportunity to model correct formation of the alphabet in a meaningful context. (By the way, if a child says no to writing their name on the story, use a sticky note on the back or take a picture of it to remember who it belongs to.)

Do not assume

Refrain from assuming what a child's drawing is or what it is about. It is up to the child to attribute meaning to their message. The educator's job is to show an interest and be an active listener and transcriber if the child chooses to share. Therefore, don't ask, "What is it?" as this might embarrass the child that you can't understand what they are communicating. As mentioned earlier, ask, "Can you tell me about it?" Not only does this give the child control, but it also asks in an open-ended way that will yield more information.

Also, do not assume a child always wants to share their story with you. They might just want to show it to you, without explanation, and that is okay. Engage and follow their cues. Even if a child can attribute meaning, it doesn't mean they will do so for all their drawings. They may just want to doodle and draw something for the sake of it, and that is fine too.

- **Writing in a meaningful context**

A few years ago, my great niece, who was four years old at the time, demonstrated this. She turned a cardboard box into a dollhouse using crayons, construction paper, and tape. She then took a piece of paper and drew a picture that represented her school, which she placed next door to the dollhouse. On that paper, she attempted to write a couple of letters to signify the name of the school. Essentially, she conveyed thoughts on paper to communicate her visions and ideas, which is fundamentally the writing process. It was child-led, it was simple, and it was meaningful. "Joy should be at the very heart of a child's writing experience. The adult's role should be to nurture this joy and bring it to life. We should be guides accompanying children on their journey to writing freedom for when children write with joy… they see the true purpose of the written word" (Bottrill, 2018). It is optimal when writing is inspired by children and connected to their play. Yet another example of how child-led play supports literacy development.

To prompt or not to prompt

With an emphasis on writing in the early years, writing in journals at a designated time has become a popular practice. While journal times and prompts are a nice invitation, keep in mind that children want to share about their worlds and their lives when it is important to them. Journal prompts don't always allow for that. "[Children] aren't interested in your purpose. They don't want to write [about a topic you picked]. It's dull and it's detached from their real experience. They may be able to do it, but their writing experience has been shallow and without the richness of motivation" (Bottrill, 2018). Journal prompts should not replace open-ended drawing. Provide blank paper and crayons around the room to allow for writing in a playful context. It will be more meaningful to children if they can draw about an experience that they truly want to share, on the timeline of their choice. It's the child's world, we need to give them the opportunity to share about it.

- **Word banks**

Create a word bank for each child using note cards and binder rings. (I usually started with five notecards per child then added more as needed.) Make this available for when children ask how to spell specific words. Word banks stayed in the writing area of my room but were allowed to go wherever needed in the learning environment. If a child, for whatever reason, wanted to know how to spell a word, instead of just telling them, I would ask them to get their word bank and I would write the word on a notecard. These were words the children were interested in, not predetermined words connecting to a theme. So, if a child has gone to an older sibling's orchestra concert, they may come to school the next day asking, "How do you spell symphony?" Instead of writing on a disposable piece of paper, write it in that child's word bank. Not only does this give an opportunity to properly model letter formation, but it creates a reference that is always there for the child, if they want to use it. What amazed me is if the child was interested in the word, and they saw me write it, they learned it and retained it. The reason? The word served a purpose in their life. Not because I said so or because a curriculum said so, but because **they** said so. The word was connected to their world, their ecosystem, so therefore, it meant something to them.

Although every child had a word bank, whether they added words to it or referred to it was up to them, based on their interest. Some children added so many words, we had to create a new word bank for them. Some only had their names written on the first card at the end of the year, and that was fine too. This was an optional activity, completely dependent on the child's interest.

Kindergarten has word walls, so shouldn't we?

A word wall is typically a big alphabet grid up on the entire size of the wall, where each letter of the alphabet has its own square. Based on the teacher's or the curriculum's discretion, words are added to the wall under their respective letter, based on the weekly theme or letter of the week. Usually during group time, the words might be "recited" as a class, or individual children might volunteer to read them on their own. Word walls are sometimes "read" every day and stakeholders marvel at how children have "learned" their words.

But do the children transfer the knowledge of those words to their everyday lives? Most likely no. Because the words are on the wall, children cannot easily access the information and bring it into their play. Instead, the words fade into the background and only serve a purpose when the class does a rote recitation of them. I often hear educators say that word walls help children learn their words. But do they? Or are they just memorized? And what purpose do these words serve in the children's lives? Instead of a word wall, find opportunities to write words in contexts that relate to the ecosystems of the children in your room. Transcribing their stories, writing their responses, and putting words in word banks are more effective and resonate way more with children, ensuring they will be more likely to transfer the words to their everyday lives.

CHAPTER FIVE

Forming the Alphabet, Without Actually Writing

The following ideas are ways of forming the alphabet without actually writing or tracing the letters. These ideas can be done at group times, play times, or transition times. Again, if doing these activities as teacher-directed experiences, ensure they do not take up child-led play time. If children seem interested, place the materials in the environment for them to play with if they choose. If this is something you have designed as an adult-guided experience and the children don't seem interested, scrap it, and move on. Also remember, not every child has to do the same letter. What letters do they want to form? Ask them, then be prepared to go with that.

These activities are not to "teach" letters, but rather extend an already existing curiosity children may have in a particular letter. This is very important; the interest needs to already be there before introducing the following experiences.

Tactile letters

Creating a letter in a tactile manner allows children to experience how it is formed without using a traceable worksheet. This can be done in a variety of ways. These experiences transcend letter formation and work eye-hand coordination and fine motor strength as well.

- **Corkboard and push pins**
  Place a letter formation on a corkboard and use pushpins to form the letters. If you are reluctant to use push pins, try using golf tees. Think of the pressure it takes to push the items into the corkboard and how it develops proprioception and fine motor strength. Adjust your supervision according to the children's needs.

- **Playdough and straws**
  Score a letter in playdough and use cut straws to press into the playdough to form the letter. Also, roll playdough into long "ropes" and use them to create various letters.

- **Natural elements**
  Use natural elements such as rocks, shells, or leaves to form and create letters.

- **Sensory tracing letters**
  This can be done with a variety of substances such as sand, salt, cornmeal, coffee grounds, shaving cream, or even gel in a plastic baggie. (Make sure the substance you use complies with your school and licensing policies.)

Be creative. Place foil or shiny paper underneath to be revealed when traced. Use a fun apparatus to trace with, such as a craft stick or colorful wand! Keep in mind, it is okay if a child just wants to doodle or draw a picture in the sensory substance. They may have no interest in creating letters and that is fine.

Cotton swabs and paint
Write a letter and let the children dip a cotton swab in the paint to dab the letter. This can be done with the child's name as well.

Gross motor alphabet experiences
Instead of keeping the experience at the table, find ways to experience the alphabet with big body movements.

Spray bottles and water
Fill spray bottles with water and take outside. Spray the water on the side of the building to create letters. Write a letter on the sidewalk with sidewalk chalk and spray the form of the letter.

Tape letter on floor for children to walk/crawl/hop its formation
Using painter's tape, create letters on the floor and then provide arrows showing how the letter is formed. Have the children walk/ crawl/ hop in the correct formation. Write big letters outside with sidewalk chalk and do the same thing.

Why do these experiences work?

Before children can write, their bodies must be developed and ready for the task. This includes the gross and fine motor skills, eye-body coordination, and the development of the vestibular and proprioceptive systems. These develop when children have ample opportunity to move about and play; not teacher-directed movements, but child-led movement, and repetition as desired. When it comes to handwriting, it is important for adults to respect children's physical development and design settings accordingly. By providing these experiences, children can develop all aspects of physical development needed for life and school success.

WHOLE CHILD ALPHABET

CHAPTER SIX

Alphabet Knowledge Begins with Child-Led Play

"We have a terrible irony. In the name of education, we have increasingly deprived children of the time and freedom they need to educate themselves through their own means" (Gray, 2013). Play is the key element being overlooked in child development and education. So many of the needed social and emotional skills along with "desired academic outcomes" can be achieved if we just let children play. But for this to happen, it is important to acknowledge true play and protect it in early childhood. "Play must be the right of every child. Not a privilege" (Souto-Manning, 2017).

What is play?

"Play is, first and foremost, an expression of freedom. It is what one **wants** to do as opposed to what one is **obliged** to do" (Gray, 2013). Play is of the child. If it is not of the child, it is not play. The adult provides the space and opportunity for children to play and only enters upon the child's invitation. This means, children are completely leading and in control. Children design the play. Children create and implement the structure of the play. Children enforce the self-chosen rules of the play. Children decide the amount of time they play and when it ends; although, the goal is for the play to go on and on. Children are responsible for the play, including cleaning up afterwards.

Figure 18 - The Components of Play

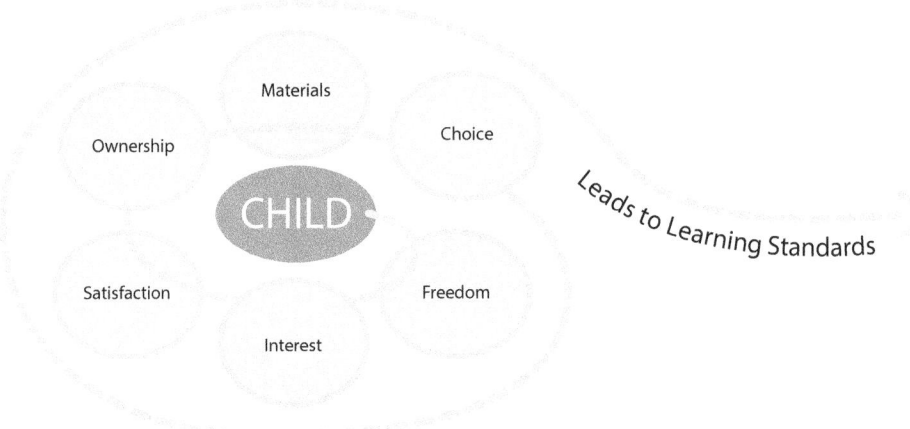

Repetition of play

It is essential for children to have opportunities to repeat their play as they desire. This is how they figure things out and improve upon what they have done previously. Children will repeat their play until they fulfill a level of satisfaction set by their own standards, which are different from adult standards. Children will be persistent and stick with the task until it is completed to their liking. Perhaps they are trying to understand something, so they continue to repeat the same dramatic play scenario. Maybe they are trying to build a structure higher than they have ever done before, so they go to the block area every day for a couple of weeks to achieve that goal. Whatever it may be, repetition is an important element when it comes to play. When adults stop play or limit repetition, they may inadvertently deprive children of important growth opportunities for the sake of "exposing them to something new" or "moving on to the next thing." We may also take away the joy of learning when we **require** them to repeat something over and over. Embrace child-led repetition and design an environment that encourages it.

What play is not

There can be a perception in education that if a child is moving while doing a lesson or engaging with a hands-on activity, it is considered to be play. But just because an activity is hands-on, doesn't make it play. Play is of the child. If the adult designs the activity, especially based on a learning standard with a specific agenda or set of instructions, it is of the adult and therefore, not play. If the adult enters the child's realm of play and tries to create a teachable moment, it is no longer of the child and hence, stops being play. When an adult requires children to participate in a certain way or puts a time limit on an experience, like rotating children through stations and making them stay there until a timer goes off, that isn't play either. We need to call these practices what they are: adult-guided playful activities, interactive learning stations, or even hands-on instruction, but not real, child-led play.

Figure 19 - Standards-Based Practice

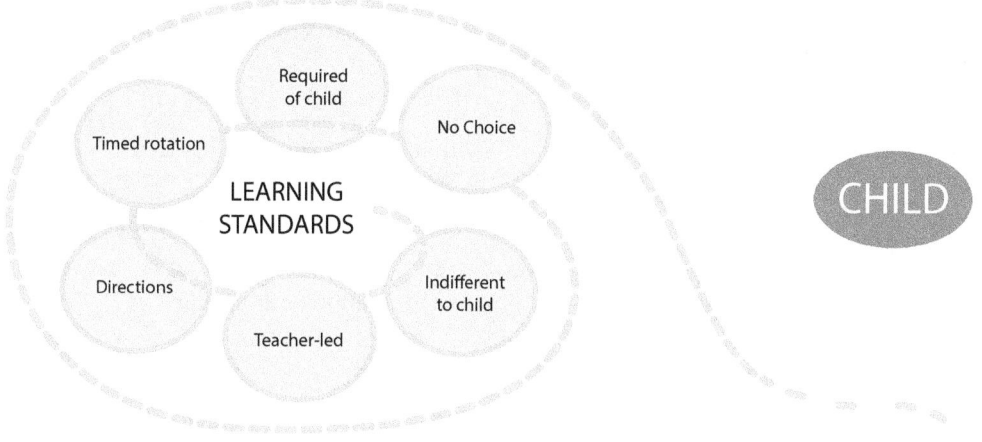

No shame in the word "play"

In an effort to get stakeholders to support play, many early educators refer to it as "play-based learning" or "hands-on learning." Play is wonderful, delightful and magnificent; it is essential and indispensable. It doesn't need to be camouflaged as something else. There should be no shame in children playing in the learning environment, especially in the name of child development. Let's give play the respect it deserves and call it by its rightful name. PLAY!

Child-Led Play vs. Hands-On Activities

"Our potential as educators is stunted when we teach from a place of pre-determined activities linked to learning outcomes that are, in turn, linked to assessments" (Pelo & Carter, 2018). There is a time and place for adult-guided, playful activities in the classroom. Ideally, these are developmentally appropriate activities and they do not overrun the daily schedule. One guideline is that every minute the adult uses for instruction should be "paid back" to the child with an equal amount of child-led play. If you are wondering about the difference between child-led play and a playful activity, Figure 20 gives a side-by-side comparison.

Figure 20

Child-Led Play	**Adult-Guided Playful Activity**
Child-driven	Standard-driven
Generates numerous outcomes	Generates limited outcomes
Free to join or leave	Degree of participation required
Materials continuously provided	Adult selects materials
Child designs and structures play	Adult designs activity
Adult observes/ enters with child invitation	Adult initiates and guides activity
Unlimited, uninterrupted time	Timed rotation or time limits
Vital for development and learning	Assists educational goals
Serves purpose of child development	Serves purpose of educational institutions

Unfortunately, in many settings adult-guided activities have taken over child-led play. This occurs for the sake of school readiness and from the fear of children being behind when they enter kindergarten. "The stronger emphasis on predetermined outcomes and the demand for more formal, teacher-led approaches to learning, particularly in phonics, have resulted in early years teaching and learning becoming increasingly like school-based learning, and this 'schoolifying' of the early childhood years goes against what we know about what enables young children to thrive" (Neaum, 2017). The paradox of sacrificing play in the name of school performance is that play naturally and organically generates the multitude of "desired academic outcomes" needed for school and life success.

Desired academic outcomes

As early care and education professionals, at some point we are most likely handed a list of outcomes perceived as a guarantee that children will be ready for school. These tend to drive teachers' practice, and nudge out play. I am not a fan of these generic lists of outcomes, as they do not respect the child as an individual, may not take child development into account, and can lead to surface teaching and skipping important foundational steps along the way. Nevertheless, desired academic outcomes are part of the reality, and influence the parameters in which we work. For this reason, we need to be able to identify all the learning taking place when children are playing, then explain how that builds strong foundations to support children in the future.

Child-Led Play and Language and Literacy

Child-led play provides so many natural opportunities to develop language and literacy. Here are some examples.

Figure 21

Child-Led Play and Early Literacy Fundamentals (The developmental skills listed coordinate with the early literacy fundamentals in Figure 2 in Chapter 1.)	
Opportunities	**Development**
Hear sounds	Phonological awareness
Converse with friends	Receptive/ expressive language
Draw	Fine motor development/ eye-hand coordination
	Writing composition/ print awareness
Read books	Comprehension
Move about room	Senses and motor skills
Manipulate materials	Eye-body coordination
Build and construct	Cognitive processing/ problem solving
Interact with friends	Social/ emotional intelligence
Choose play	Construct background knowledge of interest

Adult's Role During Play

The adult's role during child-led play is that of the observer. This requires resisting the urge to jump in to create "teachable moments." When we try and do this, we are stopping the learning by trying to teach. "We are eager to teach, and teaching, we think, means us doing something to or for a child" (Pelo & Carter, 2018). Just because you are not directing the play doesn't mean you are not an active participant. As educators, we fulfill an important role before, during, and after children's play, even if it isn't directly interacting with the child.

Figure 22 - Adult's Role During Play

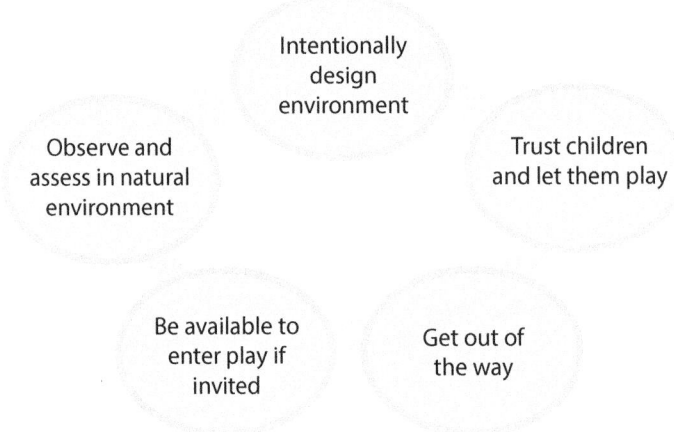

Design the Learning Environment for Play

Create an environment with the child at the center that invites and motivates them to play! Ensure the space is roomy enough and strategically designed to freely move about. Get to know the children in your class and select materials of their interest instead of ones that are theme-focused. These materials provide the opportunity for children to play and learn without adult instruction or interference, creating an environment that continuously supports children's growth and development.

Schedules and time for play

I once visited a school for teacher observations. The classrooms looked ideal, magazine-worthy, and honestly, very inviting for children's play. The only problem was the schedule. Unless a child was there before 9:00am or stayed until after 4:00pm, there was no opportunity for them to play. Because of that, the environment was almost pointless because there was little opportunity for the children to utilize anything it had to offer. A learning environment can be terrific, but unless children are granted free access to the materials and big chunks of uninterrupted time to play, the environment is not of much benefit to them.

"Time is necessary for meaningful play. When children are shuffled from one activity to the next simply because that is what the schedule says it's time to do, no one is receiving the full benefit of the experience. Many preschools chop up the day into manageable twenty-minute time blocks. Twenty minutes is not enough time for anything! It takes some children a good ten minutes just to choose what activity they want to do when they come to school each morning! So, they spend ten minutes choosing, five minutes playing, and another five minutes being told that it's time to clean up! 'Clean up?' they say. 'Clean up? I haven't even done anything yet!'" (Murphy, 2016).

How much time is needed for play? How much time is enough? "Toddlers (12 months to 3 years) could benefit from at least five to eight hours' worth of active play a day, preferably outdoors... Preschoolers (3 to 5 years) could also use five to eight hours of activity and play outdoors every day" (Hanscom, 2016). I worked at a child development center over 20 years ago where this was encouraged. We spent all day, every day outside playing, and it was awesome! If this is not possible at your setting, my professional recommendation is at least 90 minutes of uninterrupted play time in the morning and the same again in the afternoon. If your program is half day, I believe 90 minutes is still needed because the child and their needs should be at the core of all practices no matter what length the school day is. Anything less is really not long enough for children to immerse themselves into the play.

Trust Children and Let Them Play

Let's treat children like the capable beings they are. Trust them to lead their play and navigate the environment and their interactions. Will they make mistakes? You bet. Will conflict occur? Without a doubt. But what better way to learn how to handle these situations than in our care? Everything starts somewhere, including handling conflict. These skills develop through children playing and handling any situation that comes up. When the ultimate goal of play is for it to go on and on, children learn to compromise and adjust expectations to keep their friends engaged and involved. We can trust children to play and handle what unfolds.

Get Out of the Way

Rather than try to ask questions, or enrich the play, simply step back and observe. Unless the child invites you into the play, do not enter and interject. Again, this is interrupting the learning by trying to teach. "When we grab hold of children's play to wrestle it into a 'teachable moment,' we dishonor their sovereignty as thinkers" (Pelo & Carter, 2018). Thinking children's play is not enriching enough without us is not giving them enough credit. They do not need adults to guide or extend their play, they are capable of doing so on their own. Let's respect this. Design a child-centered space, invite children to play, then get out of the way.

Be Available

The most important thing an adult can do during play time is be available. Be available if the child asks for assistance. Be available to listen if a child wants to share something with you, such as a block creation or a drawing, and not be rushed. Be available to enter the child's play if they are kind enough to extend an invitation. Whatever it may be, the most important thing you can do is simply be available. (This is another reason not to pull children for small groups during play time. If you are busy conducting small groups, it prevents you from being available.)

Accepting the invitation

When a child invites you into their world, respect it. This is an honor that the child has bestowed upon you. Don't take over the experience. Treat it as if you are a guest in someone's home. When you arrive, you don't take control but instead, you follow the lead of the host and let them set the tone. Handle entering children's play in the same way. Follow their cues and let them guide the experience.

Observe, Document, and Assess

"Play is the most reliable and time-tested way to make learning visible" (Christakis, 2016). If children do not invite you into their play, this is the perfect opportunity to step back and observe them to document their interests and learning. All the evidence you need to gather can be collected during child-led play. I always kept plenty of notepads around my room to grab and write down anything I saw. I kept a portfolio for each child as a convenient place to keep documentation for future reference.

"You may have to complete those assessments, but you don't need to let that drive your practice" (Pelo & Carter, 2018). If I worked in a school that required an assessment, instead of sitting the child down to quiz them, I would go to the portfolio and pull the documentation I already gathered. This was all the evidence I needed to assess that child's progression. Having this information also helped me advocate for child-led play.

How do we use assessments?

"You are using the richness and joy of [children's] play to bring about the outcomes you need" (Bottrill, 2018). Create a user-friendly system that works for your setting and is not too complicated or time consuming. As mentioned earlier, I always recorded on paper what I observed children doing. I then went back in a timely manner to analyze the documentation. Here is a simple formula to follow:

Figure 23

I see children playing with...	
Placing books in a big basket and carrying them around the room	Building block structures and knocking them down
This is evidence of...	
• Interacting with books • Experiencing different weights • Moving their bodies about in relation to the physical environment	• Using eyes and bodies to move materials to create something • Experiencing various sounds
The resulting standards are...	
• Book awareness • Development of proprioceptive system • Spatial awareness	• Eye-body coordination • Development of visual discrimination • Phonological awareness
This will support... (relating to literacy and alphabet knowledge)	
• Print awareness • Handwriting • Reading	• Handwriting • Letter recognition • Letter sounds

Assessments to Guide Practice

Ideally our assessments should help guide our practice, not "prove" what we are doing; however, this is the world we are in. So, when completing assessments, try not to get hyper-focused on the "desired academic outcomes." Check in on them, and keep them in mind as you reflect on your learning environments and interactions. Does something need to be changed? Are the children showing an interest in something specific? Do you need to change the materials? Use your documentation and assessments for these purposes.

Play and Alphabet Knowledge

"Instead of focusing solely on academic skills such as reciting the alphabet, early literacy, using flash cards, engaging with computer toys, and teaching to tests (which has been overemphasized to promote improved test results), cultivating the joy of learning through play is likely to better encourage long-term academic success" (Yogman et al, 2018).

Go back to the early literacy fundamentals chart (Figure 2) in Chapter 1. Do you see evidence of these skills emerging when children are playing? You bet. Play does not have to connect directly to a literacy-based activity, to support literacy. In fact, a child cannot play without building skills that will support them when it comes reading and writing. The same holds true for alphabet knowledge. Think of the foundations needed to learn the alphabet: developing an interest in the letters, visual perceptual skills for letter recognition, phonological awareness for letter sounds, and physical development for writing the letters. Contrary to some beliefs, these skills emerge as they develop, rather than as they are taught. And that development happens best through child-led play.

CHAPTER SIX

WHOLE CHILD ALPHABET

CHAPTER SEVEN

Moving Forward

As a profession, we must not compromise child development and child-led play for the sake of school readiness and "getting children ahead." It is important to meet children where they are developmentally and design learning environments that support their growth and development. Digging deeper into the foundations of development helps explain what is happening in the setting and convey how those simple experiences build big skills that will support children in the future. When you can describe development and the environments that support it in detail, it helps many of the conversations you have with stakeholders.

Why do we need to know the fundamentals?

"You as an adult can adapt and change, the developmental needs of children can't" (Bottrill, 2018). A person working and caring for young children needs to understand child development, and truly appreciate the intricacies of it, and how everything works together to develop the whole child. When we grasp this (both as a profession and as a society) it shifts the focus from school readiness to building strong, solid foundations that support future life function and success – in relationships, school, work, etc. Changing this mindset depends on us as the adults, whatever our role in the child's life may be, ensuring that our expectations of children are realistic and child-centered.

It is the age-old analogy of building a house. A strong foundation is needed to support the house. If the foundation is rushed and not solidified, the house will eventually crumble and fall. If we rush children into activities they are not developmentally ready for, it is building the house with a weak foundation. If we are patient and respect the developmental process, giving children the space and time to grow and learn, they will build a substantial foundation that will support them over time.

This holds true when it comes to language and literacy. Hurrying children through activities they are not ready for is putting the child on the adults' timeline and not honoring child development. Instead of "trying to get them ahead," respect the child's developmental timeline and work with that. Yes, children eventually need to learn to read and write, but that process will be easier and more effective (when the time comes) if we give them the opportunity to develop the fundamentals needed to support those skills. Children will be more competent and capable if we honor the timeframe that is developmentally appropriate for them.

Sharing with Stakeholders

As early care and education professionals, we are in contact with not only parents and families, but also administrators, regulating agencies, community members, educators for older children, social workers and specialists. I refer to this group as "stakeholders" and it includes anyone who has a vested interest, whether actual or perceived, in what we are doing in our learning environments.

It may feel like we are being pulled in different directions by stakeholders, but it is critical that we stay rooted in our pedagogical beliefs as we establish our practices. No longer can the excuse "but [stakeholders] won't like that" be a reason to implement practices that are not appropriate for young children. It is also imperative that we are involved in the discussions pertaining to early education. If we want things to change, we need to change them. How do we initiate that change? Get the conversation going! Plant those seeds and encourage others to do the same as well. We are the experts in child development. We need to share our expertise and advocate for what is best for young children and speak out against practices and curriculums that are not developmentally appropriate.

It may seem intimidating to have a discussion with administrators regarding required classroom practices, but there is a professional way to approach them and ask to discuss pedagogy and practice. It can start with, "I attended this training that got me thinking." Or "I just read a book discussing research and high-quality practice surrounding language and literacy. Can we discuss how it compares to what we are doing in our program?" These are conversation starters, not demands. This is where change begins.

The success to any relationship is meeting the person where they are. Get to know the stakeholders and their backgrounds as well as their expectations about early childhood. View them not as barriers to our practice but as our partners who are capable of learning more about the early years. Don't shy away from conversations, instead, seek opportunities to discuss pedagogy and practices about young children in a positive and enlightening way. Be the expert in child development. Speak with passion and be convicted in your beliefs. It is as simple as that.

Focus on Child Development, Not School Readiness

"Early childhood is not school readiness" (Wardle, 2018). The purpose of the early years of life is to discover and learn about the world and how to function in it, not get ready for kindergarten. When engaging in conversations with stakeholders, shift the focus away from school readiness and onto child development.

Confidence in your knowledge of child development will support you in these discussions. Being able to explain the intricacies of it helps drive home the truth of solid foundations to support future life endeavors, especially when it comes to language and literacy. Stakeholders are excited to see children read and write. We are too! However, it is our job to share in detail how that develops. Instead of just saying 'visual perception skills,' discuss form constancy, visual closure, and figure ground and how those develop and support reading. Instead of saying 'fine motor skills,' talk about how the vestibular and proprioceptive systems support writing and how lots of boisterous movement is needed for those to develop. Sharing in-depth information helps people respect how child development supports all aspects of language and literacy and understand the importance of learning environments that support child-led play.

> *Rest assured, they will be okay*
>
> If children develop self-regulation, self-control, and can follow directions and get along with their peers, they will be successful in school. A child with "academic" knowledge that lacks these skills will have difficulty functioning in the classroom. So, how do we ensure that children have the skills they need to be successful? Provide plenty of opportunity for child-led play.

Debunking the myths

Here are four common "myths" we may face, and ways to debunk them, as well as suggested talking points for each one.

The Myth of School Readiness

The myth
"Children need to be ready for kindergarten. Part of them being ready is being able to name all their letters. If we don't spend time on that in the early years, they will be behind when they get to elementary school."

Debunking the myth
As a profession, it is time to move beyond school readiness and shift the mindset to solid early years pedagogy. Early childhood is about developing the whole child. It is also the opportunity for children to discover the world and learn how to function within it. This ability transcends the school years; it follows children their entire lives.

Alphabet knowledge is necessary for reading and writing, but not sufficient on its own. Literacy requires more than just knowing the letters, so we need to ensure our learning environments provide opportunities for all the other necessary skills to develop. If too much instruction is spent focused on the alphabet, it won't leave much time for strengthening the visual perception, phonological awareness, and motor skills. Creating a learning environment that encourages play and the development of the whole child will equip children with all the capabilities they need for kindergarten, more than hyper-focusing on the alphabet.

Talking points
"I know you are concerned about children being ready for school and not being behind. When it comes to literacy, it is important to remember that alphabet knowledge is an important component, but it is not sufficient on its own. There are many fundamentals that need to be developed to support reading and writing and I ensure my learning environment supports the development of those by allowing children to play. With this, they have experiences to build language, vision, phonological awareness, physical development, and an interest in reading and writing – all foundational skills needed to support alphabet knowledge as well as reading and writing. Skipping steps and spending too much time on just the alphabet does not create strong literacy skills. Also, by letting children play,

they develop self-regulation and self-control which are key components of being ready for school."

The Myth of the "Teaching Day"

The myth
"We break our program into a teaching day and before/after school care. We focus on the academic skills, including alphabet instruction, from 9am to 2pm and then let children play if they are here before or after that."

Debunking the myth
We give ourselves too much credit and play not enough when it comes to learning. Assuming children only learn from 9am to 2pm through adult instruction is showing a lack of understanding of child development. Children learn all day every day. Especially if they are playing. So, instead of a "teaching day" with adult-guided activities, design an environment that lets children play.

Talking points
"I know we are excited for children to learn new things and believe adult instruction must be in place for that to happen. Although children might learn a few things from a whole group time or small group instruction, they learn so much more from child-led play. This includes all the foundational skills needed for literacy. And just because I am not leading the experience doesn't mean I am not an active participant. I intentionally design the environment and encourage children to explore and investigate and figure things out. I follow their cues and step in only if invited; otherwise, I am carefully observing and documenting. The amount of learning that takes place during this play time far exceeds what any adult-guided activity could provide. Since children learn best through child-led play and learning is not limited to a timeframe, I am going to encourage this throughout the entire day. If children are playing, they are learning."

The Myth of Prepackaged Curriculums
(including letter of the week and handwriting curriculums)

The myth
"Our program uses [ABC] curriculum to ensure children learn all the kindergarten readiness skills needed to prepare them for academics in elementary school.

Children learn to recognize and write the letters by singing songs, creating craft projects, and tracing worksheets."

Debunking the myth

For children to learn the alphabet, the letters must connect to something in their lives. The letters that will be important in the learning environment will be unique to the children presently in the setting. Prepackaged curriculums cannot plan for that because the writers do not know those children. Children must also have opportunities to use the letters in a meaningful context; this happens best through play.

Instead of relying on a predetermined curriculum to teach the letters, change the focus to the developmental skills children need to support literacy. Design an environment that encourages child-led play for those skills to develop and grow. This approach is developmentally appropriate and will equip children with the strong foundations needed to learn the alphabet and eventually read and write.

> *Curriculum is not synonymous with quality*
>
> "We are pushing the limits of children's adaptability. We have pushed children into an abnormal environment, where they are expected to spend ever greater portions of their day under adult direction, sitting at desks, listening to and reading about things that don't interest them, and answering questions that are not their own and are not, to them, real questions. We leave them ever less time and freedom to play, explore, and pursue their own interests" (Gray, 2013).
>
> Prepackaged curriculums do not guarantee children will learn and be ready for school. Instead, they generate a system where boxes can be checked, and teaching can be "proven." It is a way to standardize teaching methods to ensure all educators are doing the same thing and all children are receiving the same instruction in the name of accountability and quality. All children deserve the right to high quality care and learning environments; however, that should not be defined by a generalized curriculum that is fueled by unrealistic academic goals. In reality, a one-size-fits-all curriculum cannot meet the needs of every child and what is developmentally appropriate for them.

Talking points

"I understand there is an overemphasis on children achieving a certain level of academic success before they enter kindergarten and if they don't, they will be behind. Because of this, there is a perceived notion that prepackaged curriculums streamline the process of learning and ensure all children will be ready for kindergarten. Unfortunately, these curriculums give a false sense of security.

Although they allow checking off boxes to provide "evidence" of learning, they do not guarantee that children develop the foundations needed for academics when the time comes. Children learn best when their environment meets their needs and personal interests, predetermined curriculums cannot provide this because they do not know these specific children. It is far more effective to design learning environments that empower children to lead their play and guide their learning. By doing so, children develop the foundational skills needed when they go to school. Therefore, I have intentionally created an environment that allows for chunks of play time for children to develop the skills they need to be capable of functioning in school.

As far as the letter of the week approach, research shows that is not an effective way to learn the alphabet. First, children must show an interest in the alphabet and realize letters serve a purpose. When this happens, children can learn multiple letters at once and not every letter requires the same amount of instruction time. It is best to follow children's cues and let their actions tell us when they are ready to learn the alphabet and what letters they want to learn. Therefore, as children are playing, I observe them and see what is important in their worlds. I provide paper and crayons in the room for them to draw. I watch for them to start writing letters on their papers. When this happens, I follow that cue. I am also available to write for them if they want to see how a letter is formed or want me to write a word. These experiences elicit opportunities for me to discuss the alphabet in a manner that is natural and organic. This approach is more meaningful and connects to what is important to children."

The Myth of Earlier is Better
(teaching children to read at an early age)

The Myth
"To ensure children are ready for academics, we teach them to read early." Also known as, "well, they have to learn anyway, we might as well teach it early."

Debunking the myth
"Reading mastery requires the integration of a huge number of different skills and is one of the most demanding cognitive tasks faced by a child" (Christakis, 2016). Yet, we expect children to learn to read at a young age, well before their language skills are adequately developed. The fear of the literacy gap has caused blurred lines between typical emergent literacy and developmental delays.

Believing children will be behind if they don't learn to read in the early years is unfounded. "Research finds no advantage in learning to read from age five" (University of Otago, 2009). Reading early only guarantees an early reader, it does not indicate a higher IQ or advancement in academics. "[Research indicates] that there is no difference between the reading ability of early (from age 5) and late (from age 7) readers by the time those children reach their last year at primary school by age 11" (University of Otago, 2009).

Talking points

"Yes, we are so excited for children to learn to read. It is a big accomplishment, but an early reader does not guarantee a strong reader. Reading requires many complex skills that move beyond decoding words. To be a successful reader, children need to develop visual perception, phonological awareness, and several physical skills as well. They also need adequate language development to comprehend all that is being read. Through child-led play, children develop all these skills, and have hands-on experiences that work all aspects of visual perception. Children hear a variety of sounds, including their peers' voices, which enhance phonological awareness. Their conversations during play elicit language development. While playing, children move their bodies in a variety of ways that build gross and fine motor skills as well as develop the vestibular and proprioceptive systems, all which support reading. Instead of skipping steps, let's be patient and allow children to build the fundamentals necessary to support literacy."

Advocating for Play

Let's celebrate the fact that play creates capable beings. If we simply encourage children to play, they will be better off and ready for school beyond measure. There is plenty of research to support it as well. Children can thrive and learn without the "academic" environments; however, they cannot thrive and learn without healthy, authentic interactions and relationships. These develop through play. Play is indispensable in the early learning environment. When it comes to literacy, child-led play provides ample opportunities for children to build all the developmental skills needed for reading and writing in school and in life.

CHAPTER SEVEN

Parents Specifically

I have a good friend who always reminds me we have the gift of discernment. She gives a visual of holding your hand in front of your heart. When somebody says something to you, you catch it and discern if it is meant to help or harm you. If it is meant to harm you, throw it away. If it is meant to help, you let it go to your heart. Sometimes, you protect your heart and let the statement go to your brain, where you say, "This is not meant to be personal, but it is something I need to hear and comprehend for my benefit or for the good of someone else."

As parents, we want the best for our children, but we may also validate ourselves based on our children's success or lack thereof. This makes us vulnerable, and we lose our discernment and let what we hear about our children go straight to our hearts. We overreact, we melt down. And the person who made us feel this way receives the brunt of our emotions. As an educator, when this happens, we need to find our discernment and protect our hearts, because what we are receiving is not personal but just a response to a parent's vulnerability.

In the book *The Importance of Being Little: What Young Children Really Need from Grownups*, Erika Christakis mentions three fundamental questions parents have for teachers: Do you like my child? Is my child normal? Is my child going to be a success? "Parents can tolerate a lot of unsettling feedback if they know that the answer to that first questions is a resounding yes" (Christakis, 2016). This is where we meet parents. This is where we begin. We build trust with parents by reassuring them that we like their child, they are fine, and they will be okay in school and life.

Parents as the Experts of Their Children

"The truth is that parents and educators are continuously learning from each other in a collaborative partnership. Acknowledging this early on can help to build a strong foundation for a trusting and responsive relationship" (Payne, 2021). I mentioned earlier that as educators, we are the experts in child development. But parents are the experts in their children. We need to invite them into our world and let them be included. We need to treat them as competent people capable of understanding child development. "Competent parents: competent to understand the intricacies of classroom life; competent to engage in dialogue across differences; competent to challenge our teaching practices; competent to shape the culture of our child care centers; competent to share, with us, the creative work of making community" (Pelo & Carter, 2018).

Reassuring Parents

Parents might ask you about how their children compare to others and if they are ahead or behind. This is the perfect opportunity to share with them the importance of play and building strong foundations to support future reading and writing. Let them know that developmentally their children are where they should be and that is great. If parents ask what they can do to get their children ahead, reassure them that rushing to teach their children academic skills is not the key to success. Instead, encourage parents to let their children play and educate them on how this builds the fundamental skills needed for literacy. If parents want specific guidance, here are some suggestions for them to implement at home.

- Lots and lots of child-led play. Encourage buying toys and materials without batteries that motivate children to play.

- Have conversations with children. With infants and toddlers, narrate the day and what all is happening. For preschoolers, ask open-ended questions that are relevant to the situation. Always give children the opportunity to fully respond and actively listen to what they have to say.

- Put the screens away. It is okay to use them to communicate with distant family or to show children how to look up information, but avoid using them to pacify time. This includes car rides, restaurants, and going to the store. Instead of plugging the child in, let them be present and experience all the sounds and sights the environment has to offer.

- Read real books and have lots of conversations about them. Give reassurance that children may want to stay on one page and talk a lot about it. Toddlers may want to randomly flip through the book. Some children may want to repeat a book and read it over and over and over. That is great and all part of the literacy process. Encourage family members to follow their children's cues and enjoy the experience.

- Have blank paper and crayons available! Scribbling is important and way more effective than children drawing on coloring sheets. Let children draw and show an interest in their creations!

CHAPTER SEVEN

WHOLE CHILD ALPHABET

Change Begins with Our Pedagogy

As you incorporate new ideas and strategies into your work, don't get overwhelmed. Remember, everything starts somewhere. Find a starting point and begin taking baby steps from there. In time, you will look around and realize your learning environment reflects how young children learn best, and supports them in learning to function in the world.

"What's the right thing to do when you believe in one thing and are required to do something else?" (Pelo & Carter, 2018). How do you feel about what you have read in this book? Do you feel challenged? Overwhelmed? Excited but not sure where to start? Whatever it may be, dig into that and address it. Then figure out what you are going to do with the information going forward. What changes do you want to make in your learning environment? Will there be barriers? If so, how can they be removed? This may include having conversations with key stakeholders to ensure everyone is on the same page. Providing research and reassurance will be critical steps in this process.

Part of growing as a professional is continually learning and letting your pedagogy evolve. There was a time I believed themes were the only way to go. I also had my fair share of activities based on letter of the week, when I was teaching. But when you know better, you do better. As I started attending training sessions and reading countless books, my professional beliefs began to change. We are allowed that. We develop and grow as educators. Were my early practices ideal? Not really. Did I have the best intentions? Absolutely. Did I make changes as my knowledge expanded? You bet! That is growing as a professional. Everything starts somewhere, including our professional practices. This book is intended to help you grow and move forward.

Make the Difference

"As early literacy is vital for children's later learning, equally vital is practitioner's knowledge and understanding of young children, child development, early years' pedagogical approaches, and practitioner's subject content knowledge, which in terms of literacy includes a good understanding of what leads into literacy" (Neaum, 2017). We are the experts in child development. We must keep advocating for practices rooted in research and fact. It is not always easy, but it is necessary. Knowing the unrealistic expectations put upon children, we must keep working on their behalf. I hope this book gives you information needed to make changes that will truly benefit the children you serve, as well as confidence to have the brave conversations necessary to advocate for what is best for young children. Let's move ahead with perseverance and determination. Children's movement, growth, development and well-being are all causes for celebration. Child-led play and educators and environments that support it, are joyful and essential ingredients. You make a powerful difference in children's lives, with every choice you make, every day. Here's to new actions, new conversations, new opportunities and new growth for children, and for teachers.

WHOLE CHILD ALPHABET

Bibliography

American Academy of Pediatrics. "Infant Vision Development: What Can Babies See?" Healthy Children, January 5, 2012. http://healthychildren.org/English/ages-stages/baby/Pages/Babys-Vision-Development.aspx

Beck, C. "What Are Visual Spatial Relations?" The OT Toolbox, June 8, 2021. https://www.theottoolbox.com/what-are-visual-spatial-relations/

Blakeslee, S. "Babies Learn Sounds of Language by 6 Months." *New York Times*, February 4, 1992.

Bottrill, G. *Can I Go and Play Now? Rethinking the Early Years.* London: Sage, 2018.

Boyd, K. "Vision Development: Newborn to 12 Months." American Academy of Ophthalmology, June 8, 2020. https://www.aao.org/eye-health/tips-prevention/baby-vision-development-first-year

Brown, J. (n.d.). "Experts Reveal the Truth About When to Worry About W Sitting." *Lemon Lime Adventures.* https://lemonlimeadventures.com/when-to-worry-about-w-sitting/

Carlson, F. *Big Body Play: Why Boisterous, Vigorous, and Very Physical Play Is Essential to Children's Development and Learning.* Washington, DC: NAEYC, 2011.

Ceceri, K. "Early Reader/ Late Reader: Does it Matter?" ThoughtCo, July 3, 2019. https://www.thoughtco.com/early-reader-late-reader-does-it-matter-1833103

Christakis, E. *The Importance of Being Little.* New York: Penguin Books, 2016.

College of Optometrists in Vision Development. (n.d.). "Learning-Related Vision Problems." www.covd.org: https://www.covd.org/page/learning

Connell, G., & McCarthy, C. *A Moving Child Is a Learning Child.* Minneapolis: Free Spirit Publishing Inc., 2014.

BIBLIOGRAPHY

Curtis, D. *Big Body Play: Why Boisterous, Vigorous, and Very Physical Play is Essential to Children's Development and Learning.* Washington, DC: NAEYC, 2011.

Curtis, D. "Seeing and Supporting Children's Active Bodies (and Minds)." *Exchange,* 54-58, 2018.

Derman-Sparks, L., Edwards, J. O., & Goins, C. M. *Anti-Bias Education for Young Children and Ourselves.* Washington, DC: NAEYC, 2020.

Editors of Teaching Young Children. *Learning about Language and Literacy in Preschool.* Washington, DC: NAEYC, 2015.

Eide, B., & Eide, F. *This Mislabeled Child: Looking Beyond Behavior to Find the True Sources - and Solutions - for Children's Learning Challenges.* New York: Hachette Books, 2006.

Epstein, A. S. *The Intentional Teacher: Choosing the Best Strategies for Young Children's Learning.* Washington, DC: NAEYC, 2014.

Esparza-Young, E., Sarmiento-Arribalzaga, M., & Harris, S. B. "Nurturing Early Literacy with Nursery Rhymes from Around the World." *Early Years,* 17-20, 2018.

Gibbs, M. *Fine Motor Skills... Write Out of the Box! A Guide to Fine Motor Development for the Whole Child.* North, VA: Gibbs Consulting, Inc., 2015.

Gray, P. *Free to Learn: Why Unleashing the Instinct to Play Will Make Our Children Happier, More Self-Reliant, and Better Students for Life.* New York: Basic Books, 2013.

Hannaford, C. *Smart Moves: Why Learning is Not All in Your Head.* Salt Lake City: Great River Books, 2005.

Hanscom, A. J. *Balanced and Barefoot.* Oakland: New Harbinger, 2016.

Heffron, C. "Developmental Skills: Crossing the Midline." The Inspired Treehouse, July 5, 2015. https://theinspiredtreehouse.com/developmental-skills-crossing-the-midline/

Hirsh-Pasek, K., & Golinkoff, R. M. *Einsten Never Used Flash Cards*. Emmaus, PA: Rodale, 2003.

Kranowitz, C. S. *The Out of Sync Child: Recognizing and Coping with Sensory Processing Disorder*. New York: Penguin Group, 2005.

Lazarus, D. R. "Optometrists Network." April 6, 2020. https://www.optometrists.org/vision-therapy/guide-vision-and-learning-difficulties/vision-and-learning-difficulties/

Mays, J. H. *Your Child's Motor Development Story: Understanding and Enhancing Development from Birth to Their First Sport*. Arlington: Sensory World, 2011.

McKay, R., & Teale, W. H. *No More Teaching Letter A Week*. Portsmouth: Heinemann, 2015.

Murphy, L. *Lisa Murphy on Play: The Foundation of Children's Learning*. St. Paul: Redleaf Press, 2016.

Murphy, L. *Lisa Murphy on Being Child Centered*. St. Paul: Redleaf Press, 2020.

NAEYC. *Developmentally Appropriate Practice in Early Childhood Programs Serving Children from Birth through Age 8*. Washington DC: NAEYC, 2009.

NAEYC. "Advancing Equity: Position." 2019. NAEYC: naeyc.org/resources/position-statements/equity-position

NAEYC. "DAP: Defining Developmentally Appropriate Practice." 2020. NAEYC: naeyc.org/resources/position-statements/dap/definition

Neaum, S. *What Comes Before Phonics?* London: Learning Matters, 2017.

Nebelong, H. "Nothing Ventured, Nothing Gained: Exploring Children's Playscapes." *Exchange*, 54-56, 2017.

NEPS, Report Writing Group. "Visual Perception." 2015. National Educational Psychological Service (NEPS): https://assets.gov.ie/41301/e3632f9137544262b40d7e0c5e9a3604.pdf

BIBLIOGRAPHY

NYPL Staff. "Culturally Diverse Nursery Rhymes to Share." August 12, 2020. The New York Public Library: https://www.nypl.org/blog/2020/08/12/culturally-diverse-nursery-rhymes

O'Connor, A., & Daly, A. *Understanding Physical Development in the Early Years*. Abingdon: Routledge, 2016.

Olsen, J. Z., & Knapton, E. F. *Get Set For School: Readiness & Writing, Pre-K Teacher's Guide (Handwriting without Tears)*. Cabin John: Get Set for School, 2016.

Payne, K. "Connection Not Catch-Up." *Teach Early Years*, 12-13, 2020.

Payne, K. "EYFS reforms - How inclusive are they for children with SEND?" May 20, 2021. Teach Early Years: teachearlyyears.com/a-unique-child/view/eyfs-reforms-how-inclusive-are-they-for-children-with-send

Pelo, A., & Carter, M. *From Teaching to Thinking: A Pedagogy for Reimagining Our Work*. Lincoln: Exchange Press, 2018.

Plank, E. *Discovering the Culture of Childhood*. St. Paul: Redleaf Press, 2016.

Ramirez, N. F. "Why the baby brain can learn two languages at the same time." April 15, 2016. The Conversation: https://theconversation.com/why-the-baby-brain-can-learn-two-languages-at-the-same-time-57470

Safe to Sleep. (n.d.). "Tummy Time." Safe to Sleep: https://safetosleep.nichd.nih.gov/resources/providers/downloadable/tummy_time_image

Schickedanz, J. A., & Collins, M. F. *So Much More than the ABCs: The Early Phases of Reading and Writing*. Washington, DC: NAEYC, 2013.

Schickedanz, J. A., & Collins, M. F. "Alphabet Letter-Name Knowledge." *Teaching Young Children*, 11(5), 2018.

Schneider, C. *Sensory Secrets: How to Jump Start Learning in Children*. Siloam Springs: Concerned Communications, 2001.

Souto-Manning, M. "Is Play a Privilege or a Right? And What's our Responsibility? On the Role of Play for Equity in Early Childhood Education." *Early Child Development and Care*, 187, 2017.

Spracher, M. M. "Learning About Literacy: SLPs Play Key Role in Reading, Writing." April 1, 2000. ASHA Wire: https://leader.pubs.asha.org/doi/10.1044/leader.SCM.05082000.1

University of Otago. "Research finds no advantage in learning to read from age five." December 21, 2009. University of Otago: https://www.otago.ac.nz/news/news/otago006408.html

Wanless, S. B., & Crawford, P. A. "Reading Your Way to a Culturally Responsive Classroom." *Young Children*, 8-13, 2016.

Wardle, F. *Oh Boy! Strategies for Teaching Boys in Early Childhood*. Lincoln: Exchange Press, 2018.

Yogman, MD, FAAP, M., Garner, MD, PhD, FAAP, A., Hutchinson, MD, FAAP, J., Hirsh-Pasek, PhD, K., & Golinkoff, PhD, R. M. "The Power of Play: A Pediatric Role in Enhancing Development in Young Children." *Pediatrics: Official Journal of the American Academy of Pediatrics*, 142(3), 1 – 16, 2018.

Yopp, H. K., & Yopp, R. H. "Phonological Awareness is Child's Play!" *Young Children*, 12-18, 2009.

www.ingramcontent.com/pod-product-compliance
Lightning Source LLC
Chambersburg PA
CBHW080412230426
43662CB00016B/2382